Lectionary Stories *for* Preaching *and* Teaching

Cycle C

for the Revised Common Lectionary

A Compendium of Stories from
StoryShare
a Component of **SermonSuite.com**
from CSS Publishing Company

CSS Publishing Company, Inc.
Lima, Ohio

LECTIONARY STORIES FOR PREACHING AND TEACHING

FIRST EDITION
Copyright © 2012
by CSS Publishing Co., Inc.

Published by CSS Publishing Company, Inc., Lima, Ohio 45807. All rights reserved. No part of this publication may be reproduced in any manner whatsoever without the prior permission of the publisher, except in the case of brief quotations embodied in critical articles and reviews. Inquiries should be addressed to: CSS Publishing Company, Inc., Permissions Department, 5450 N. Dixie Highway, Lima, Ohio 45807.

For more information about CSS Publishing Company resources, visit our website at www.csspub.com, email us at csr@csspub.com or call (800) 241-4056.

ISBN-13: 978-0-7880-2675-1
ISBN-10: 0-7880-2675-5

PRINTED IN USA

Table of Contents

Introduction	9
Advent 1 *Luke 21:25-36; Psalm 25:1-10* Larry's Story	10
Advent 2 *Malachi 3:1-4* Preparing the Way	13
Advent 3 *Philippians 4:4-7* There Is No Good Reason	16
Advent 4 *Luke 1:39-45 (46-55)* Packing Christmas	18
Christmas Eve / Day *Isaiah 9:2-7* Christmas Crazy	21
Christmas 1 *Colossians 3:12-17* Harmony	24
New Year's Day *Ecclesiates 3:1-13* Hunting for Life	27
Epiphany of Our Lord *Matthew 2:1-12* Journeymen	30
Baptism of Our Lord / Epiphany 1 / Ordinary Time 1 *Luke 3:15-17, 21-22; Psalm 29* Hovering Over the Waters	33
Epiphany 2 / Ordinary Time 2 *1 Corinthians 12:1-11* Not So Dumb Idols	38

Epiphany 3 / Ordinary Time 3   40
Luke 4:14-21
Her First Sabbath

Epiphany 4 / Ordinary Time 4   43
Psalm 71
Whine and Cheese

Transfiguration of Our Lord   45
(Last Sunday after Epiphany)
Luke 9:28-36 (37-43)
Transforming Light

Ash Wednesday   48
2 Corinthians 5:20b—6:10
Darkness Before the Light

Lent 1   53
Romans 10:8b-13
Aren't You Ashamed?

Lent 2   55
Genesis 15:1-12, 17-18
As Clear as the Milky Way

Lent 3   59
Isaiah 55:1-9
God's Dinner Bell

Lent 4   62
2 Corinthians 5:16-21
The Ugliest Man in the World

Lent 5   66
Psalm 126
Panic and Recovery

Passion / Palm Sunday   69
Luke 22:14—23:56
Passionate Sense

Maundy Thursday   73
1 Corinthians 11:23-26
Julia Gilbert Changes Love Feast Among the Brethren — Twice!

Good Friday   76
John 18:1—19:42
Betrayal in the Third Grade

Easter Day   80
Acts 10:34-43
Eyewitnesses

Easter 2   82
Acts 5:27-32
We Must Obey God

Easter 3   85
Acts 9:1-6 (7-20)
The Good Little Girl

Easter 4   89
John 10:22-30
Who Do You Trust?

Easter 5   91
Revelation 21:1-6
Everything Old Is New Again

Easter 6   93
John 14:23-29
The Great Starvation Experiment

Ascension of Our Lord   96
Ephesians 1:15-23
The Eyes of the Heart Enlightened

Easter 7   99
John 17:20-26
In All His Glory

Pentecost Sunday   102
Acts 2:1-21
I'd Like to Thank...

Holy Trinity Sunday 104
John 16:12-15
Guided on the Path

Proper 4 / Pentecost 2 / Ordinary Time 9 108
1 Kings 18:20-21 (22-29) 30-39
Give Me an S...

Proper 5 / Pentecost 3 / Ordinary Time 10 112
1 Kings 17:8-16
Oh God... Please Don't Make Me Go!

Proper 6 / Pentecost 4 / Ordinary Time 11 115
1 Kings 21:1-10 (11-14) 15-21a
The Mayor's Wife

Proper 7 / Pentecost 5 / Ordinary Time 12 119
1 Kings 19:1-18
7 - 7-7-77

Proper 8 / Pentecost 6 / Ordinary Time 13 123
Luke 9:51-62; Psalm 77:1-2, 11-20
Confidence in Crisis

Proper 9 / Pentecost 7 / Ordinary Time 14 125
2 Kings 5:1-14
Being Helped in Spite of Himself

Proper 10 / Pentecost 8 / Ordinary Time 15 128
Luke 10:25-37; Psalm 82
Where Have All the Good Samaritans Gone?

Proper 11 / Pentecost 9 / Ordinary Time 16 131
Luke 10:38-42
Housewarming Warning

Proper 12 / Pentecost 10 / Ordinary Time 17 135
Hosea 1:2-10
I Have Loved You...

Proper 13 / Pentecost 11 / Ordinary Time 18 141
Luke 12:13-21
Then What Will You Do?

Proper 14 / Pentecost 12 / Ordinary Time 19 143
Isaiah 1:1, 10-20
Is Anybody Listening?

Proper 15 / Pentecost 13 / Ordinary Time 20 146
Isaiah 5:1-7
Donnie's Plant

Proper 16 / Pentecost 14 / Ordinary Time 21 150
Jeremiah 1:4-10
God Searches for a Spokesperson

Proper 17 / Pentecost 15 / Ordinary Time 22 153
Jeremiah 2:4-13
Thirsty for Living Water

Proper 18 / Pentecost 16 / Ordinary Time 23 156
Philemon 1-21
Terminally Shy

Proper 19 / Pentecost 17 / Ordinary Time 24 161
1 Timothy 1:12-17
The Biggest Sinner

Proper 20 / Pentecost 18 / Ordinary Time 25 163
1 Timothy 2:1-7
Hero

Proper 21 / Pentecost 19 / Ordinary Time 26 165
Psalm 91:1-6, 14-16
Be Not Afraid

Proper 22 / Pentecost 20 / Ordinary Time 27 168
2 Timothy 1:1-14
Caught Not Taught

Proper 23 / Pentecost 21 / Ordinary Time 28 171
Luke 17:11-19
The Outsider

Proper 24 / Pentecost 22 / Ordinary Time 29 175
Psalm 119:97-104
Deontologize the Principle of Parsimony

Proper 25 / Pentecost 23 / Ordinary Time 30   178
2 Timothy 4:6-8, 16-18
Looking Ahead

Reformation Day   180
Jeremiah 31:31-34
A Change of Heart

All Saints Day   183
Daniel 7:1-3, 15-18
Crazy Dreams

Proper 26 / Pentecost 24 / Ordinary Time 31   186
2 Thessalonians 1:1-4, 11-12
Small but Mighty Faithful

Proper 27 / Pentecost 25 / Ordinary Time 32   189
Luke 20:27-38
The Wrong Lens

Proper 28 / Pentecost 26 / Ordinary Time 33   192
Luke 21:5-19; Isaiah 12
In That Day

Christ the King / Proper 29   194
Jeremiah 23:1-6
What's the Stick For?

Thanksgiving Day   196
John 6:25-35
Bread

About the Authors   199

If You Like This Title...   203

Introduction

Since you are reading this, you probably preach on a regular basis. It is important to not only bring God's word to the members of your congregation but to help make the gospel of Christ engaging and thought-provoking.

Most people know that Jesus, the Master Storyteller, very often used stories and parables to make an important point to his listeners about God's kingdom. Following his example, we know that helping people to understand God's word through the telling of a story not only provides additional interest in a message, but also makes that same message easier to understand.

Over the years, CSS has published thousands of relevant, interesting, and inspiring anecdotes and stories to season a pastor's sermon. Not only has CSS produced numerous books to aid pastors in this important part of ministry but CSS also has a weekly online service called **StoryShare**, a component of **SermonSuite.com**, that was created to bring preachers the most timely and relevant illustrations possible. This edition of stories and anecdotes, gleaned from **StoryShare** for Cycle C, are written to dovetail with the readings from the Revised Common Lectionary and will serve you well as extended illustrations or in many cases, stand-alone sermons.

It is our hope that the stories in this book will not only assist you, the pastor, in your preaching but will also help you throughout your ministry.

The editors at CSS Publishing Company, Inc.

Advent 1
Luke 21:25-36; Psalm 25:1-10
by Sandra Herrmann

Larry's Story

On the fiftieth anniversary of D-Day, I asked my congregation to tell me their stories of World War II. This is Larry's story, just as he told it to me. It's appropriate for the reading for this Sunday — and I promised him I would pass it on, so that what he went through would never be forgotten or glossed over.

I'm not sure I should even tell you this story. It's too hard to hear, and I don't want to hurt you. But since you insist, I will.

It was 1945, and I was 21 years old — a man, not because of my age, but because of the fighting I'd seen in the war. The platoon I'd served in had had a lot of bad luck, and I had only one friend left. We'd been transferred into a new outfit, because we weren't going to get any new guys anytime soon.

We were told there was a camp a few miles up the road and we were needed there, but no one prepared us for what we were about to see. When we got there, there were men holding onto the fence, watching us. But they were barely alive. They looked like skeletons.

Bodies were stacked up like cordwood. There were piles of them all over the camp. Most of them were like skeletons. They were mostly naked, so you could see every bone in their bodies. Even the living looked like skin stretched over the bones.

You may have seen the picture, but the pictures don't — can't — tell the story. The worst of it was the smell. The smell hit us first and then we began to realize what we were seeing. It was horrible. Even now, I can't tell this without crying.

We were sent to go through the barracks, to find the living if we could. I went into one barrack where bodies were laying three across on the bunks that rose in tiers. It looked like they were all dead and the stench was so awful I turned to go — but then I heard a sound. I turned back and saw a hand feebly raised on an upper bunk. I climbed up and there was a man lying between two dead bodies. He could barely move; he couldn't even speak because his mouth was so dry.

I picked him up to take him down from the bed, and he was as light as a feather. He was about as tall as me, but he weighed about what a child would weigh and I got him down easily. I told him we would take care of him and started toward the door. He turned his head away from the light, just as the sergeant blocked the doorway.

"Don't bring him outside. The light is too bright out here. Most of the men haven't seen the light of day for too long. He could die."

I laid him down and propped him against a wall near the door so that he could get used to the light a little at a time and went back to see if there were any more men still alive in that hellhole. (I'm sorry, there is no other word for it — it was like entering hell.)

There was one other man left alive in that building, but he died when we tried to feed him. They'd been without food for so long that eating anything beyond a kind of gruel was too much. We killed a few with kindness before we caught on that they needed to take everything very slowly.

We gave them a little water, and had to hold back on it so their mouths and throats could soften enough to swallow. It was like getting them used to the light — we had to move very slowly... and some of them died in the process.

We brought in equipment to bury the bodies. They had no identification on them, so we had no idea who they were or where they were from. These people's families would never hear that they died at Bergen-Belsen but maybe it was just as well. To know that someone you knew had died like that, how could you stand it?

I'm sorry. I thought I could tell this without crying, but evidently not. It was horrible. We had no warning of what we were about to see and the young man I'd found, who weighed the same as a child, who looked at least forty — he was the same age as me. We were both 21.

Larry, how could you even live after that — after such a horrible experience?

(Larry laughed a heavy laugh.) Well, when I came home I bought an old Indian bike (a brand of motorcycle) and went on a road trip. I rode out west into the Badlands and then back. I had to get a job by then. And on weekends, I would ride all over. I'd open her up to see how fast she could go. I was fearless… had a bad accident once. My arm never did heal right. The truth is, I didn't care if I lived or died for a long time, until I met the woman who became my wife.

She saved my life and my sanity. We've been married nearly fifty years now. She knew how to soothe me when the dreams woke me up. It's been a few years now since I've woken up from one of those dreams.

I don't think I could stand up and tell this story to the congregation. But if you could, then people would remember — if you could stand to do it.

Advent 2
Malachi 3:1-4
by Peter Andrew Smith

Preparing the Way

Muriel rolled the vacuum cleaner down the aisle toward the closet. There was still dust and glitter here and there on the carpet, but she kept moving. Enough was enough. After an hour of cleaning she had done all she was going to do. Any places she missed vacuuming would just stay missed. She had done her part and more. Besides, no one would see the mess once when they were sitting in the pews.

"Need some help?" Carol asked, holding a tray covered in tin foil.

"No, I'm fine." Muriel tossed the attachments on top of the vacuum as she closed the door. "They hit you up for something too?"

"Yes," Carol said, as she lifted the foil. "They asked me to bring cookies for the children after the concert."

"They seem to be asking everyone for something this year," Muriel said. "I haven't had kids in Sunday school for years, but the teachers keep asking me to do things. Sometimes I think I'm too old to be involved with pageants and concerts."

"I remember teaching you in Sunday school, so imagine how I feel," Carol said. "But we all need to do our part, don't we?"

Muriel wiped her brow with her sleeve. "I wish more of the parents would help out. When our kids were Sunday school age we didn't ask everyone to do things for the events we held."

"When we had more people in the church it was easier to find more help. Things are different now, for sure." Carol took a cookie from the tray and offered it to Muriel. "But then again, I never had to work outside the home when my children were young. I wouldn't want to try to work full-time and raise a family."

"Too true. I found it hard enough just working two mornings at the clinic." Muriel took a bite of the cookie. The sweet taste reminded her of the pageants she was in when she was a girl. There were always treats and hot chocolate after they performed the Christmas concert for the congregation. "Carol, you make the best cookies. I remember running backstage to get them when I was in Sunday school."

"You're very sweet, dear," Carol said, as she steadied herself against the table. "But with the way my sight is going I won't be able to help out with baking for many more years. I'm going to miss being able to do this for the Sunday school."

"You must really like baking."

"I wouldn't say that I actually like it, but after all these years I don't mind it."

"Really? Then why do you do it?"

"Why, to help out of course," Carol said as she pulled a cookie from the tray and chewed on the corner. "It's my way to be John the Baptist."

"Sorry?"

Carol laughed as she looked at Muriel's face. "You weren't here when Reverend Ambrose was pastor, were you, dear?"

Muriel shook her head. "He was before my time."

"He preached a sermon during Advent on the passage in Malachi about God promising to send someone ahead to prepare the way for the good things that were coming." Carol broke her cookie in half and gave part of it to Muriel. "He challenged us to find ways we could help make the good news happen, like John the Baptist did when he prepared the way for Jesus."

Muriel put the piece of cookie in her mouth. "What does that have to do with baking?"

"What were some of your best times in church?" Carol asked.

"The pageants in December," Muriel said without a pause.

"I like to think that in some small way my cookies made great things happen for the children who were a part of the Sunday school. I don't think that I did anything major, but I hope I helped prepare the way for the Holy Spirit to move and make an impression on the young minds and hearts."

"You certainly helped make Sunday school special for me." Muriel kissed Carol on the cheek. She opened the door to the janitor's closet and started to haul out the vacuum cleaner.

"I thought you were all finished," Carol said.

"There are some places I think I missed," Muriel replied, as she went back to work getting things ready for the Sunday school concert that night.

Advent 3
Philippians 4:4-7
by C. David McKirachan

There Is No Good Reason

Joy's not easy. We usually get it mixed up with happiness or satisfaction or some other form of having a time somewhere on the better side of terrible. But joy, real hammer-down, open-the-turbo, wide-eyed, out-of-breath, explosion-of-flavor, jaw-dropping, kick-down-the-gate, shake-and-giggle, get-hoarse-singing joy is rare in our lives. It scares us because it's kind of nuts. It worries us because we stop being efficient and can't really stick to the agenda — we're too busy overflowing to be neat and organized.

I grew up in the last ice age. It used to be cold on Christmas Eve. It used to snow with great regularity. Drifts that covered things like fire hydrants and front porches were to be expected. I grew up in an insane church. We all knew this. We were kind of proud of it. The primary proof was the open-air bus trip we always had on Christmas Eve. Yeah, you heard me — open-air. I mean, if you're going Christmas caroling how else would you get from here to there except in an open-air bus?

How cute you might say — how delightful. Have you ever tried to sing with a 30-mile-an-hour wind blowing snow into your mouth? This wasn't Currier and Ives. This was a hare-brained scheme hatched in the fevered brain of our minister of music and my crazy father, the pastor. They sat down and planned this debacle to express the injunction from the fourth chapter of Philippians: "Rejoice, again I say, rejoice!"

My response to that at the time was, "Wow! God planned this?" I was five or six. My response as a twelve-year-old was, "You've got to be kidding. What's the real reason?" Any sane person could see there was no reasonable justification for this. The only mystery greater than why anyone would plan such a wingnut idea was why the bus was packed every year.

But let me tell you (cynical twelve year olds aside), when we came in from the blizzard, huffing and puffing, we glowed. We had our hot Dr Pepper (who ever thought of that needed help), said a prayer, and went home to put on our church clothes for the midnight candlelight service. I mean, how else would you get ready for the wonder and the mystery of Randall Thompson's *Alleluia* by candlelight? "And the word became flesh and dwelt among us."

Joy! Yup. Nuts.

Merry Christmas.

Advent 4
Luke 1:39-45 (46-55)
by John Sumwalt

Packing Christmas

My soul magnifies the Lord, and my spirit rejoices in God my savior, for he has looked with favor on the lowliness of his servant. — Luke 1:46b-48a

There was once an old woman who lived in a big, old Victorian house filled with the many treasures she had collected over her 89 years — antique furniture, original paintings, a twelve-piece setting of rose-patterned china sent by her late daughter from Hong Kong, a silver tea set, and many more lovely knick-knacks and keepsakes that had been given to her by family and friends.

When the time came that the she could no longer care for herself, her relatives arranged for her to have an estate sale. They told her that every thing had to go because there wasn't going to be much room in the nursing home.

Then after almost all of the her lovely things had been sold, they packed her few remaining clothes and possessions into a big leather suitcase and an old chest of drawers that she had inherited from her grandmother. It had traveled with "grandma" across the plains in a covered wagon during the Oklahoma land rush. The woman also insisted on taking a very large battered wooden trunk, which she said her father had crafted from scrap lumber when he worked at the trunk factory in Kansas City. It had been a Christmas gift to her mother in 1913, the year before she was born. The trunk had originally been painted black, had once been dark as coal, or so she said, but was now faded and streaked with gray like the old woman's hair. They packed the suitcase, the chest of drawers, the trunk, and the old woman into the minivan and set out for her new home.

When they arrived at Pine Valley Manor they expected that she would be very sad; that, as it had been for many others before her, this would be a difficult day with many tears. But she was smiling as they walked in the door behind the cart that carried her suitcase, the old chest of drawers, and the cherished trunk. She was absolutely beaming, as if this was one of the happiest days of her life.

Just then the load on the cart shifted and the contents of the trunk spilled out onto the floor. There were packets of carefully folded bright-colored Christmas wrapping paper; bundles of aged Christmas cards tied with string; a caroler's songbook; hand-knit monogrammed Christmas stockings; a string of red, green, blue, and white lights; a porcelain angel in a yellowed plastic bag; more than a dozen Christmas ornaments in original boxes; and a miniature nativity set carved from ivory.

"Oh my," the old woman laughed, "I guess I need to travel lighter." She knelt down, picked up the tiny baby Jesus figure, and gently laid him in the manger. "You are all I need," she whispered, as if speaking to him alone. Then she gathered up the remaining pieces of the nativity set — the stable, the donkey, the cow, the sheep and lambs, shepherds, wise men, camels, Mary, and Joseph — and tucked them all into the pockets of her coat. And turning to her nephew, the one who had driven the minivan, she said, "Jerry, why don't you take the trunk home. And if you don't want it, give it to one of your sisters. Maybe they can get some use out of some of this old stuff." She laughed again as Jerry helped her to her feet.

One of the aides who had come to escort the old woman asked her how she could be so happy on a day like this. She said, "You haven't even seen your room yet," in a tone of voice that suggested that it wasn't really very nice.

The old woman smiled and said, "Oh, I don't have to see it. I know it will be all right. I've learned to be content wherever I am. God has been so good to me. I feel so blessed."

All those years she had been packing Christmas in her heart, the kind of Christmas you can take with you wherever you go.

Christmas Eve / Day
Isaiah 9:2-7
by John Sumwalt

Christmas Crazy

It seems like everyone goes a little bit crazy at Christmastime in our part of the world. There is the pressure to get all the Christmas shopping done and the added tension of crowded stores, crowded highways, jammed parking lots, and fender benders. People race each other for parking spots and often things are said that are downright un-Christmas-like.

People are cranky. Arguments break out over how much money to spend — or little things like whose parents' house do we go to first — or what gift to get for dear Aunt Gertrude who always says, "You don't need to get me anything," but would never speak to you again if you didn't.

In one family, Mom and Dad were arguing all day about various Christmas-related things. That night when their little daughter knelt down by the bed to say her Christmas prayers, she prayed, "Forgive us our Christmases, as we forgive those who Christmas against us."

One year I was over at the grocery store on Christmas Eve morning laying in supplies for the army of relatives that was coming to our house for Christmas maneuvers the next day. Did you know that everyone in the world goes grocery shopping on the day before Christmas? I finally found a place to park about two miles from the store. And if that wasn't bad enough, the congestion inside the store was like a NASCAR event. There were so many shoppers with shopping carts (by the way, there are some people who should not be allowed to drive a shopping cart!) that they had security guards with pointer lights and whistles directing traffic between the aisles.

I don't know about you, but when I go grocery shopping I like to stop and ponder what I'm going to buy, compare prices, check the labels for transfat and the percentage of mouse droppings and insect wings before I make my selection. There was no stopping and pondering that morning. It was like driving on the interstate. While I was stopped in front of a cheese display trying to decide between a nice smoked Gouda from France and a specialty cheese from Spain made with sheep's milk and jalapeño peppers, three shoppers with carts packed to overflowing swooped in and pinned me against the display case.

It was worse when I got to the checkout line. There were carts stacked up like semis at a weigh station. My line snaked all the way back to the Sugar Pops in the cereal section. When I did finally get close enough to the checkout counter to read the headlines on the tabloids (did you know that Arnold Schwarzenegger was an alien?), a very nice old woman with two items in her cart squeezed in front of the guy ahead of me, smiling all the while and saying it was all right because the girl behind the checkout counter was her granddaughter (I'm not making this stuff up). Then we all got to listen for ten minutes while they made plans for Christmas dinner.

In the car on the way home from the grocery store I found myself singing Christmas carols and feeling strangely sad. Tears came into my eyes — it seemed just out of the blue. I thought to myself, what is this about? I have every reason to be happy. All of our family is coming for Christmas — and then I knew, no, not all of our family. Dad wouldn't be there. Almost all of us have loved ones in heaven who are especially missed at Christmastime. It is not uncommon to feel blue or depressed at Christmas.

In the midst of all of the joys of the Christmas season there are so many reminders that fill the heart with sorrow. Many of us live with empty places around the Christmas tree where loved ones once laughed and rejoiced with us. Christmas can be as difficult as it is joyful.

In his Advent study, *The Cradle and the Star*, Reginald Mallett recounts the sudden death of his mother-in-law one Christmas. Many people expressed concern about the sudden shadow that fell over the season. The one person who was most helpful wrote to the family and said: "Do not think of the shadow that this sorrow casts over your Christmas. Think rather of the light that Christmas sheds on this sorrow."

There is so much sorrow and heartache in the world, children starving in Darfur, mothers and fathers and grandmothers and grandfathers dying of AIDS in Africa leaving thousands of AIDS orphans. Every time we hear of another gunshot victim in the inner city or another young person dying from heroin in the suburbs (heroin in the suburbs! Lord, help us!), we wonder, is there really any hope for our world?

The prophet Isaiah wrote these words of hope to his nation at a time when they were drowning in the darkness of their own evil ways: *"The people who walked in darkness have seen a great light; those who lived in a land of deep darkness — on them light has shined."*

The light comes in most unexpected ways. Do not despair when it seems the darkness is about to drive out the last shred of hope; the light will come. There is something about this Jesus baby that creeps into our hearts and transforms all of the craziness in our world.

Christmas 1
Colossians 3:12-17
by C. David McKirachan

Harmony

    I was five. At that age I was not the Clydesdale that I later became. I was skinny and, like most five year olds, short. It was Christmastime and the chancel choir was doing its usual job of blowing the socks off of anyone who wasn't stone deaf. Pine Street Presbyterian Church is a cathedral in center-city Harrisburg, Pennsylvania — gothic arches, stained glass, dark wood, seating for hundreds create an atmosphere of soaring possibility. Add to the mix a moose of a pipe organ and an ambitious minister of music with an imagination and a sense of humor and talent and you've got a music program that touched a lot more than eardrums.
    The big "C" choir was somewhere around fifty voices. When it held forth I was entranced. I sang in the cherub choir. We wore big, black bows and stood on the steps down in front of the chancel. The chancel choir's loft was a balcony above the chancel, up there, up where angels perched. They sang in harmony.
    My family sang around the table and in the car and in the living room and at the beach. We were a singing bunch. Mom sang soprano, Daddy sang tenor, Fred sang baritone, Susie and Margaret vacillated between alto and soprano and tenor. I just sang. We sang in four parts or seven, depending on the song and the enthusiasm level. Harmony was always my favorite thing. The layering of voices, each doing something different, creating out of all that difference a new and miraculous glory. It was better than pie (and we have some amazing pie makers in our family).

But the chancel choir did harmony that was different. It was the sperm whale of singing. It had momentum and a depth that could pick up a mob of people and carry them in its gut. It turned that stained-glass-studded barn of a nave into the hold of a ship. Everyone there was cargo — and we were carried and delivered onto the threshold of heaven. Harmony...

So the minister of music asked my parents if I could sing a solo. I heard that. I'd done that before. But then he said "... with the chancel choir." My five-year-old jaw dropped. My mother looked at me (at this point in my life, I was still shorter than she) and said, "David, would you like to sing a solo with the chancel choir?"

I don't remember the anthem. It was a Christmas carol arranged for choir. I was the cute factor. But I also had that clear child's soprano. I don't remember rehearsing. I do remember coming into the loft on that Sunday. Everyone was in there, all in their chancel choir robes. I still had to wear the bow. They were in the pews that angled around the organ console. I had to get down front, next to the director. They'd put a box there for me to stand on, so I could see over the rail — down, down to the nave, down to all the upturned faces.

My mother had taught me to say, "Excuse me" if I stepped on toes. As I scooched down the pew in front of the basses I stepped on a lot of toes, so I started saying, "Excuse me." One guy picked me up and passed me along to the next. The bass on the end deposited me on the box. I said "Thank you." That got a laugh. I don't remember the specific song. But I do remember the harmony. I sang... and I loved it. I loved adding my voice to the glory. I loved joining and weaving and lifting and being part of something so beautiful it overflowed and cascaded down to the rest of the world.

J.B. Phillips' translation of this passage from Colossians includes the phrase "remembering that as members of the one body, we are called to live in *harmony*." If I envision the kingdom of God it is just that — many voices, all singing, each in their own part, an anthem of thanksgiving and hope, in harmony.

Merry Christmas.

New Year's Day
Ecclesiates 3:1-13
by Frank Ramirez

Hunting for Life

> *To every thing there is a season, and a time to every purpose under the heaven: A time to be born, and a time to die; a time to plant, and a time to pluck up that which is planted; A time to kill, and a time to heal; a time to break down, and a time to build up....* — Ecclesiastes 3:1-3 KJV

For many people in America it's a toss-up whether Thanksgiving Day or the Black Friday shopping extravaganza is the biggest holiday. For many, having football all weekend long makes it a special time. And for most people it is a four-day weekend, from Thursday through Sunday, giving everyone time for feasting — and recovery! Of course students are glad to be out of school the whole time. In the midst of it all are people giving thanks to God, the creator of all good things, for all the good things that have been created.

But for those in middle and western Pennsylvania it's a five-day holiday weekend, and the last day, the Monday after Thanksgiving, is the best day. It's the time when a family tradition is handed down from one generation to another, when in the pre-dawn hours folks go out into the dark and get out into the brisk late autumn air, when finally what everyone has been dreaming about for weeks finally comes true.

Because in that part of the world, the Monday after Thanksgiving is the first day of deer season. It's a school holiday. And for most folks, it's a work holiday. Long before the season officially starts at dawn, mothers and sons, fathers and daughters, good friends and close family, both those that live nearby and those who travel back from out of state, are trudging through the snow to a treasured deer stand, newly repaired in the days just past, to wait in the dark for the season to begin.

No doubt some, perhaps those who live in cities, or who disdain hunting, would be alarmed that this is such an important event. However, the deer that are harvested will eventually end up in freezers, feeding families through the long winter months, whether in good economic times or bad. In bad times, the venison, which is leaner than almost every other meat and is healthier as well, will grace many grateful tables. (Nor does it have a gamey flavor as it does in some parts of the country. The deer have been eating corn all summer long. Indeed, some farmers plant corn not to be harvested, but to feed the deer.)

Not only those hunters benefit. Venison is often donated to food banks and distributed to those who are having a hard time making ends meet. It is always gratefully received. The bounty is passed on.

There are those who do not eat meat at all, but otherwise, those who purchase beef, chicken, or pork at the meat counter of their grocery store, should bear in mind there is not moral difference between animals raised for dinner, and those which are hunted to grace the table. Perhaps there is a moral advantage to eating the deer, for unlike animals that are raised in factory farms, the deer roam freely over the valleys and hills of the Appalachian hills of Pennsylvania.

Most importantly of all, the hunters are actually strengthening the herd. In most places in Pennsylvania, deer have no natural enemies. Sickly animals are as likely to survive as healthy ones. A herd whose growth is unchecked spreads sickness more easily. Not only that, but an over-large herd means that trees are destroyed, some plants are eaten out of the environment, and other animals are squeezed out of the habitat. The death of some deer strengthens the overall population.

Most of us, when reading the third chapter of Ecclesiastes, may understand that there is a time to be born and a time to die, but may struggle with the Teacher's lesson that there is a time to kill as well as a time to heal. But in God's creation death brings life. There is a great circle and cycle that we are a part of, being fed, and in our time feeding the earth as our dust returns to the dust from which we came. And isn't that at the heart of our faith? Doesn't the death of Jesus give life to all of us? Small wonder that at least in a small way our death, the death of the deer, the harvesting of plants which results in their death as well, in some way or another brings life, and healing, to the world.

The author, Frank Ramirez, is the pastor of the Everett Church of the Brethren. He is from Los Angeles and has never hunted in his life, but has come to appreciate the place this ritual holds in the lives of the people in his church. Each year he leads a special blessing of the hunters on Thanksgiving Sunday.

Epiphany of Our Lord
Matthew 2:1-12
by Keith Hewitt

Journeymen

After eleven years of writing Christmas plays for our church — eleven years of re-reading the biblical account, eleven years of reading and re-reading histories of that time and place, eleven years of listening to Christmas CDs by Trans-Siberian Orchestra or Mannheim Steamroller in August just to set the mood — I have learned a couple of things. One, no matter when I start, I will always be writing the last scene in mid-November, just before we start practicing. Two, my favorite characters to work with are the Magi.

Over the years, just to keep things fresh, I have written about the nativity from the viewpoint of almost everyone involved, from the angels to the innkeeper, but I keep revisiting the Magi. They are the ones who speak to me across 2,000 years of history, and I believe it's because the journey of the Magi is sort of a scale model of our spiritual walk, our journey toward God.

Matthew tells us that the Magi were first attracted to the appearance of a star that foretold the birth of a new king — in other words, something shiny caught their eye. Many of us start our own journeys for the same reason; something happens to catch our attention, something happens that says "God" to us, and we are drawn to it to learn more.

The Magi's journey did not take them in a straight line. They followed a path that must have seemed reasonable to them, only to find that reason took them to a dead end instead. Reason alone would not take them to the new king — and reason alone will not take us to a relationship with God. I believe we don't have to abandon reason, but if we are going to draw closer to God there comes a time when we must admit that there is something more, something *beyond* reason… like faith.

Faith is not unreasonable but I suppose you could say it is non-reasonable. It supplements reason but does not depend on it. In the words of one of the characters in this year's play, "Reason will only take you so far… faith will carry you the rest of the way." To move forward, we have to be prepared to step beyond reason.

The Magi found Jesus where they did not expect him. We also may encounter God in places we do not expect — in the words of a friend or the actions of a stranger, a moment of quiet realization as we look up at the infinite night sky or watch the world being reborn at sunrise. Our journey may take us through church and we *may* find what we're looking for there — but we may also connect with our Creator in other ways and other places.

Once the Magi did find Jesus, Matthew tells us they were filled with joy; they worshiped him, opened their treasure chests, and surrendered the contents to the child and his parents. When we finally make that connection, when our own walk with God brings us face-to-face with the reality of his love, there is that moment of understanding… and joy — the moment when our heart soars and we say, "Now I get it." And it's at that moment that we surrender ourselves to him and offer up what treasure we have — nothing as pedestrian as gold, frankincense, and myrrh, but gifts that truly matter: love, praise, and a willingness to do what God wants us to do.

Finally, we are told that the Magi's journey after they found Jesus was not a straight line home — rather, they were urged to follow a more circuitous route that would keep them from encountering King Herod's wrath along the way. How often have we found that our own journey, after discovering God, has been a meandering one? The road beyond that first encounter — that first moment of acceptance, is seldom straight — it takes twists and turns we did not expect and even leads us down into some valleys, but will always bring us back to the summit, if we stay on the path.

I'm no wise man — ask my wife or friends — but when I look at their journey to Jesus, and then at mine, I feel a connection to them, for we have followed the same road… just not over the same terrain.

Baptism of Our Lord
Epiphany 1
Ordinary Time 1
Luke 3:15-17, 21-22; Psalm 29
by Craig Kelly

Hovering Over the Waters

The wind whipped through the hair of everyone at the gathering. It was something of a dual blessing — it cut the humidity a bit, plus it blew away some of the stagnant, pungent odors that had hung over them. At least their nostrils wouldn't be stinging as much during the ceremony. Many of the seventy-some people gathered gave silent thanks to God for that.

There weren't many chairs on the flat rooftop where they were gathered. The building on which they were standing was once a school, so they were able to find a few chairs that were still intact. They kept those for the elderly and the nursing mothers in their group. The rest resigned themselves to standing for the ceremony. It was worth it, though. Any small bit of happiness and celebration was a welcome change these days.

One of the men stepped forward to address the crowd. He was carrying an old Bible with a faded leather cover, its pages rippled from having been wet. He carefully turned the fragile pages to the book of Luke.

"I baptize you with water, but he who is mightier than I is coming, the strap of whose sandals I am not worthy to untie. He will baptize you with the Holy Spirit and with fire," he said, his voice slightly trembling. Moving his finger down the page a few verses, he continued, "Now when all the people were baptized, and when Jesus also had been baptized and was praying, the heavens were opened, and the Holy Spirit descended on him in bodily form, like a dove; and a voice came from heaven, 'You are my beloved Son; with you I am well pleased.' " He closed his book and walked back into the crowd as several heads nodded in silent assent and approval, others adding a quiet "Amen."

Another man, apparently the leader, stepped in front of the congregation, his own ripple-paged Bible in hand. "Thank you, Brother James, for that reading from the Word. I would like to add another few passages before we finish the service today. Now as you all know, since those terrible days water has become an inescapable part of our lives. Everywhere we look since the typhoon, water is everywhere. It is now brown and dirty with dirt and waste and oil and blood. We still see dead animals and dead human beings floating around us even today. Water has made life hard for us all." Everyone nodded, some wiping tears from their faces.

The speaker opened his Bible as he continued. "But we serve a God who is no stranger to the water. Genesis 1:2 says, 'The earth was without form and void, and darkness was over the face of the deep. And the Spirit of God was hovering over the face of the waters.' In Psalm 29, King David asserts that 'The Lord sits enthroned over the flood; the Lord sits enthroned as king forever.' God is no stranger to the flood, my brothers and sisters.

"And just as we have seen water bring death here in Manila, we also know that water also brings life. We cannot live without it, as we have seen with many of our fellow Filipinos suffering for lack of clean water to drink. Out of water can come both death and life. There is no better illustration of this than what we are about to do today. As our sister Maricel enters the waters of baptism this morning, she is demonstrating openly to all what has already taken place in her heart. She has buried her old, sinful nature with Christ, having nailed it to his cross. As she is lowered into the water, we acknowledge with her that she has been buried with

Christ, sharing in his death. Out of this water will come another death."

The pastor's eyes now brightened, a wide smile forming on his face. "But as she rises, brothers and sisters, as she rises, she is sharing in the resurrection of Christ. She is rising to newness of life! Because our Lord defeated death and sin, she too will rise with Christ! She is now in Christ and is a new creation; the old has gone — behold, all things have become new!"

The congregation erupted in spontaneous applause. As they began to make their way to a large, aluminum basin filled with water, they began to sing a song of praise, thanking God for what was to come.

The congregation all had played a part in this ceremony. All the healthy adults had gone on a water fast for the day, using the heavy-duty water filters given to them by a humanitarian agency to filter enough water to baptize Maricel. They all felt it was a sacrifice well worth making. God's command to baptize did not end just because of a flood. Besides, everyone needed something to celebrate.

"Maricel, would you please come forward?"

A young, dark-haired woman, slender almost to the point of being gaunt, stepped out of the congregation. She was dressed in a dark T-shirt and sweat pants. She didn't want to wear her Sunday best, knowing what condition those clothes would be in by the time the service was over. She stepped up to the basin and removed her shoes and socks. She then stepped into the basin and into the water, still having a slight tint of brown despite being filtered. The pastor and a church elder stepped up to the basin, standing on either side of Maricel. Linking hands, they joined together in prayer.

"Heavenly Father," the pastor began, "we thank you and praise you for what is about to happen here today. We thank you that you have chosen Maricel and set her apart as one of your children. We thank you for the sacrifice your Son made on the cross so that she, and all those who call you Lord, could share in the new life you provide for us. We pray that as Maricel is lowered in the water, you would seal in her heart that she truly is dying; her sin, her me-first life is being left in the water, dead. And as she rises out of the water, we pray that just as the Holy Spirit descended on your Son after his baptism, you would fill Maricel to overflowing with your Spirit, living and working through her. And as this body stands as a witness to this, we pray that we would always be lifting her up in prayer, helping her to live out this new life to which you have called her. In all these things, we give you praise and thanks, in the name of Jesus Christ, your Son. Amen." The "amen" rippled through the congregation, joining their prayers with the pastor's.

The pastor turned to Maricel, smiling. "Maricel, have you repented from your sins, accepting Jesus Christ as the Lord and Savior of your life? Have you invited him into your heart?"

"Yes, I have," Maricel said, smiling even as she trembled slightly. The wind and the water were giving her a slight chill, even in the Manila heat.

"Then, based on your confession of faith, as the Lord commanded, in the presence of these witnesses, I baptize you in the name of the Father, and of the Son, and of the Holy Spirit."

Together, the pastor and the elder guided Maricel into the water. As she descended, Maricel felt the water flowing up her body, covering her legs, then her hands and arms and chest, rising up, washing over her ears and mouth and eyes and nose, until she was all the way under. She was buried.

A moment later, she could feel strong yet gentle arms drawing her up. As she emerged from the water she opened her mouth, filling her lungs with air, alive again. She was reborn. Everyone applauded and cheered, praising God. Maricel, still dripping wet, laughed and raised her hands to the sky. Throwing her wet head back, she began to shout.

"Praise you, God! Praise you, Lord Jesus! You are truly King over the flood! You are the King of Manila!"

Epiphany 2
Ordinary Time 2
1 Corinthians 12:1-11
By C. David McKirachan

Not So Dumb Idols

Paul had a lot of gall. How dare he tell perfectly wonderful members of the Corinthian church that they had worshiped dumb idols "... as their impulses led you." Impulses! Well! Obviously these were not good Presbyterian folk or he was gravely mistaken.

But gratefully, this has no meaning for our people. Our idols aren't dumb. They're smart and verbal.

There's the idol of Convenience. It precludes the necessity for sloppy human interaction with gifts like drive thrus and email and instant messaging and shopping on the internet. Hey, quick and easy... Sounds like a litany to me.

Then there's Comfort. It allows us to grow fat and ignorant as well as insensitive with gifts like super-sized, non-nourishing trans-fat-polluted fast food, remote controls for TV's that hypnotize and sell rather than inform and challenge, and people who act like preachers and insist on supporting our prejudices rather than challenging our idolatries. Where's the flag in your church?

There's the Bottom Line. It insists on ignoring social injustice and environmental destruction for the sake of the short run "practicalities" of business (see above).

There's Instant Gratification. It tells us we never have enough and it insists the good life can be had with plastic. It instructs us to guzzle everything because the object is obviously Convenience, Comfort, and the Bottom Line rather than any sort of appreciation.

And then there's Me First...

Nope, they're not dumb or stupid. And we, if we are in the Spirit, are supposed to have given them up.

But I think too often we get to the latter list of gifts for the building of the body while we still worship the idols that entangle our culture and our lives. No wonder we have a hard time acting like the Body of Christ. We're still pagan.

Paul knew this and the Lord knew this. We'll always be a mixed bag. It's not the idols that are dumb. It's us. I guess that's why love and not perfection is the "more excellent way." God must love us. It's the only reason we weren't deep fried long ago.

But does this mean I have to give up the heated seats in my car?

Epiphany 3
Ordinary Time 3
Luke 4:14-21
By Sandra Herrmann

Her First Sabbath

> *Then Jesus, filled with the power of the Spirit, returned to Galilee, and a report about him spread through all the surrounding country. He began to teach in their synagogues and was praised by everyone.... When he came to Nazareth, where he had been brought up, he went to the synagogue on the sabbath day, as was his custom. He stood up to read, and the scroll of the prophet Isaiah was given to him. He unrolled the scroll and found the place where it was written: "The Spirit of the Lord is upon me, because he has anointed me to bring good news to the poor. He has sent me to proclaim release to the captives and recovery of sight to the blind, to let the oppressed go free, to proclaim the year of the Lord's favour." And he rolled up the scroll, gave it back to the attendant, and sat down. The eyes of all in the synagogue were fixed on him. Then he began to say to them, "Today this scripture has been fulfilled in your hearing."*
> — Luke 4:14-21

Josh was digging out a hole to plant the lilac bush he'd just brought home when the lady next door approached the fence.

"You must be the new neighbor," she said.

"Yep. We just moved here from Wisconsin. My wife got a promotion with her publishing company." Joshua extended his hand.

"Welcome to the neighborhood. I'm Rachel Kaufman. Your wife is that beautiful blonde I've seen coming and going?"

"That would be the one. Kristen. And your husband is the fellow with the black curly hair?" Josh ran a hand through his thinning ash hair.

Rachel giggled, and said, "Yes, Joshua's the envy of every man for fifty miles."

"No fair!" Josh made a face. "We have the same name, and he got all the hair!"

They laughed as Rachel Kaufman proudly introduced her children — Daniel, Leah, and Gideon. Each of the children had large brown eyes and the curly hair of their father. And they all laughed easily. Josh could hardly wait to tell Kristen what good neighbors they had.

As the weeks passed, he would tell Kristen stories about their encounters, but somehow she was never out in the yard when the Kaufmans were, so they remained strangers. Until, that is, Rachel caught Kristen one morning as she was leaving for work.

"I've been looking forward to meeting you, Kristen. I have a little something for you." And so saying, she presented a plastic bag with slices of something coated with nuts. "I hope you'll enjoy it."

Kristen eyed the bag. "What is it?"

Rachel smiled. "*Monlach* — it's poppy seed, honey, and walnut candy. A special dessert for Purim."

Kristen blinked. "What's Purim?"

"Our Jewish spring holiday. I made a huge batch this year, so we still have some left. Enjoy."

And off she went, with a quick wave as she hurried back to the house.

That evening, Kristen brought the unopened bag to Josh. "Want some?"

Josh opened the bag and popped a piece in his mouth. "Mmm! Honey and nuts. Hey, this is great stuff," he said around a second piece.

Kristen blushed.

"What?" Josh asked, while digging for a third piece of the candy.

"I didn't try them. Are they really tasty?" At the look on Josh's face, her blush deepened. "Well, I didn't know what was in them. I don't know anything about Jewish food."

41

"Well, get over it honey. I've accepted their invitation for Sabbath dinner this Friday. It'll be a great experience!" At her look of incredulity, Josh laughed and kissed her. "Daniel says that the Sabbath is just a good time with family, friends, and good food. It's supposed to be fun."

But for the rest of the week, Kristen was anxious, not knowing what to expect. She didn't want to embarrass herself or the Kaufmans, so she got on the internet to check out what the Sabbath was all about.

When Friday came, she made a point of leaving work early. Sabbath, she had learned, began at sundown, and she didn't want heavy traffic to make them late.

Joshua Kaufman answered the doorbell. "*Shabbat shalom!* That means, 'a good and peaceful Sabbath.' Come in."

Kristen couldn't resist his warmth. And when they were ushered to the dining room, she was amazed at the beautifully decorated table. There were even candles on the table.

"Do you do this *every* Friday?" she asked, savoring the smell of roasting chicken.

Joshua answered her. "Yes, though we put out the good china for our guests. The Torah tells us that the Sabbath is a day in which to celebrate, to eat good food, and to include our neighbors in that celebration. After all, 'The joy of the Lord is our strength.' "

Kristen gasped. "We just read that in our Bible study at church! That was our memory verse for the week. That's the perfect touch for my first Sabbath experience."

Epiphany 4
Ordinary Time 4
Psalm 71
By C. David McKirachan

Whine and Cheese

New findings in research are always fun to read. The latest information on heterosexual relationships indicates that men and women probably shouldn't talk about their relationships to solve their problems. Since they speak two different languages and their priorities in relationships are different and their personal anxieties are based on different dynamics, the more they talk the further they move apart.

Great, so where does that leave the marriage therapy industry?

Anyway, one of those personal anxiety dynamics these experts mentioned was shame. Evidently men are much more worried about failure and shame than women are. Women are worried about fear and isolation. Hmmm… so Psalm 71 was probably written by a guy, "Let me never be put to shame."

I read this Psalm and I thought it whined a lot. So I thought as I sat in profound, well-adjusted judgment. Where is this person's faith? Why don't they just get off their insecure butt and get moving? Then I read the article about personal anxiety dynamics. Strangely, it embarrassed me. Gee, am I a guy or what? I value my willingness to say and do things that push the envelope. I value my sense of security and boldness. I value my reputation for being a little nuts. I was embarrassed at being discovered. I was ashamed of my whining.

Yep, guilty as charged. Periodically, I positively wallow in the muck of shame and ooey, gooey self-pity. Pooor meee.

I thought it had to do with my regression as an integrated personality back to the infantile desire to be treated as a vulnerable and needy being. I could live with that. And now I find out it's a guy thing. I asked a few women what they thought of this finding. They all responded "Duuhh…" I think they knew it all along. So much for ground-breaking research.

I shared it with another pastor, male by physiology, who responded, "Yep, I always liked that Psalm." This bothered me more. Aren't we supposed to be open and beyond such petty needs and desires? Of course. But we aren't and we never will be. So this is just an honest expression of some guy's natural inclination to worry about shame and to whine about it. Don't you think God knows we whine? Who made him so well adjusted?

Great, so now I'm ashamed about being so limited in my relationship with God. You'd think after all these years I could have learned that God accepts me as I am. I don't deserve God's acceptance. Oh, how can I be an effective pastor…

I think I'll serve a little cheese with this latest whine and have a party. But I'll make sure to invite the Lord. God knows he puts up with a lot. Or is it she?

Transfiguration of Our Lord
(Last Sunday after Epiphany)
Luke 9:28-36 (37-43)
by John Smylie

Transforming Light

The Cursillo movement has evolved in many different directions over the years. Cursillo is a short course in Christianity and, at its best, it assists those who participate in becoming leaders in their local church. Though it was originally a Roman Catholic renewal experience, it has expanded over the years into other mainline denominations. Originally the movement served men only; eventually it grew to serve women as well and now some variations of it include weekends for teenagers as well as young adults.

I knew a young man who attended one of these variations of the Cursillo movement. At the time, he was a teenager. He was already recognized as a leader among his peers, being a three-sport varsity athlete, an honor roll student, and a Boy Scout. He was a pretty quiet kid and his life was not as easy as it may have appeared on the outside. His parents divorced when he was just a little boy. As a child he bounced back and forth between their two homes. Every Tuesday night and every other weekend spending the night with his father, the rest of the time he was with his mother. Like most children whose parents have divorced, he longed for his parents to get back together and yet the reality was very clear that that would never happen. He didn't want to see that.

Eleven years after his parents divorced, his mother remarried. Though on the surface he tried to appear pleased for his mother, internally this change was difficult for him. Now it was abundantly clear that his parents would never get back together. Two years after his mother remarried, when he was age fifteen, he was invited to participate in a "Happening" weekend. A few of his friends had experienced a "Happening" weekend before him and had encouraged him to attend. They described the experience as awesome. His mother and stepfather also encouraged him to go on the renewal weekend. They both had experienced the movement and believed he was ready for the mountaintop experience it so often provides those who participate in it.

He went and gave himself fully to the experience.

When he returned home on a Sunday evening, he was riding high while at the same time tired from all the activities and excitement. It was clear he had been stretched by the teaching and challenged by the call to commitment. He came home from that experience with a new excitement for his faith. He had been on a mountaintop and he couldn't sleep that night. He wanted to talk and listening to him was a wonderful experience for his mother and stepfather. They were delighted to see how the Lord had brought God's light to him through the faithful community that served him during the weekend.

At the end of the conversation that Sunday night he looked toward his stepfather and said, "There's something I've got to tell you, but I'm not ready to tell you right at this moment."

His stepfather replied, "Whenever you are ready I'm here to listen to you."

Three days later the boy's stepfather began to wonder if whatever it was that his stepson desired to share was ever going to come to the light of day. Another day passed when finally the boy told his stepfather, "I'm ready to share with you now."

The two of them went to a room in the house where they could be alone and undisturbed.

The boy seemed to be struggling. He was naturally a quiet kid and it seemed as if the sharing was a great leap of faith.

He held his head down as his stepfather sat across from him waiting for him to speak. Finally, he looked up close to tears and with a pained expression on his face said, "You know, when you married my mom, that was really hard for me. I want my mom to be happy but it was really hard to have you come into my life and my family. What I realized over the weekend was that God has brought you to my life."

This vulnerable and intimate sharing stunned his stepfather. He didn't know what to say, perhaps there was nothing to say. He simply received the gracious words of his stepson, words that demonstrated maturity far beyond the fifteen years of the boy's life and expressed his gratitude by taking the boy into his arms and surrounding him with a strong embrace.

It seems to me whenever we encounter the living God, whenever we experience the radiant face of our Lord Jesus Christ, whenever we dare to come in to the real presence of the holy, we are changed and strengthen to brighten the real and challenging everyday world in which we live, just like this young man who was strengthened by God's transforming light and love overcame himself by reaching out beyond himself.

Ash Wednesday
2 Corinthians 5:20b—6:10
by Larry Winebrenner

Darkness Before the Light

Remember that thou art dust and unto dust thou shalt return.

Imposition of ashes reminds us of our mortality and immortality at once. Those very words used in the service when imposing ashes were used by the Lord to Adam when he sinned in the Garden of Eden.

But there's another reminder we should take to heart. Traditionally, the ashes come from the palms burned on the previous year's Palm Sunday. Christ marched victoriously into our lives. Although we executed him and laid him in the tomb "unto dust to return," Christ broke the bonds of sin we had tied him with, conquered death, and, through him, God revoked the sentence of death.

No wonder Paul cried, "We entreat you on behalf of Christ, be reconciled to God. For our sake he made him to be sin who knew no sin, so that in him we might become the righteousness of God" (2 Corinthians 5:20b-21).

Yet, the words should encourage us beyond this eternal reward. They should remind us that Christ accomplished this in the temporal world. We need not wait for eternity to have hope. God is at work in the world now.

Annie and Dowling Martin found this true in the darkest day of their lives back in 1928. When they married in 1899, Annie's father let the couple work a piece of land called variously Cavenders Branch or Cavenders Swamp. The couple farmed the land, built a barn, and lived in it while building a house.

They were dirt farmers in the poorest county in South Carolina but managed to enlarge the fields and raise nine children. Edna was the youngest girl, and she cared for Robert, three years younger than her, while the parents and other eight children worked the fields.

Like many six year olds, Edna was fascinated by fire. She especially loved the way those little sticks of wood with the red tip burst into flame when rubbed against a rough surface. And she found a whole box full of them! What fun to strike a match. Throw it down. Strike a match. Throw it down. Strike a match. Throw it down. The problem came when a loose piece of wallpaper caught fire. She didn't know what to do. She lugged Robert out into the yard and started screaming, "Mama! Mama!"

Dowling was in a far field plowing corn. The older boys were hoeing peanuts. The girls were picking beans, some to sell in town on Saturday, and some to can for the winter. Annie was in her flower garden. She sometimes made as much as a dollar on Saturdays selling flowers in Walterboro. But the flower garden was on the side of the house opposite to the side where the barn stood.

By the time Annie realized Edna was screaming for her, not playing at being mommy to Robert, Dowling had seen smoke rising from the house. He left horse and plow and raced across the furrows toward the house.

Frank, the eldest son, heard his sister's screams. When he looked over toward her, he saw flames through the open door. He ran toward the open door when Annie yelled, "Stop Frank!" He didn't want to stop. His only earthly possession was a banjo. He wanted to save it

"My banjo, Mama," he said.

"Banjos can be replaced," she said. "Sons can't."

By the time Dowling arrived, the family was standing in a group watching the flames shooting out the windows, licking the eaves. "Didn't nobody do nothin'?" he asked, despair in his voice.

Annie stood there, tears in her eyes. All their clothes. All their furniture. All their dishes and cookware. All their mementos collected over the years. All their Christmas decorations so carefully packed away. All their photographs. Even their family Bible. Everything. She turned to her husband. "Do nothin'? Dowling, what'd we do? Form a bucket brigade with two water buckets and a well? Ain't nothin' gonna stop them pine boards from burnin' once they start." She took her pruning shears and walked back to the flower garden.

That night the family slept in the barn.

"What are we going to do now?" asked Annie, knowing that Dowling didn't know any more than she did.

"We'll have to move to the city where I can find work." Doubt filled his voice.

"God will show us a way." Then Annie was very quiet.

Someone once said it's darkest just before the dawn.

No one could have coaxed the Martin family into believing that dawn was about to break. But with the house gone, it was almost impossible to raise nine kids. And Annie was pregnant again. Dowling had to find work of some kind. His brother Charley, living in Beaufort, told Dowling there was work for carpenter's helpers in Beaufort.

Dowling's first inclination had been to go to Charleston or Savannah to find work. But big cities were scary... unknown. Beaufort wasn't that much larger than Walterboro. Still, it had an adjacent marine base that helped the economy. And Dowling did know something about carpentry work. He built his own house and barn. He had helped neighbors build theirs, too.

So the Martins loaded the old farm wagon with tools, chickens, a sow, and kids. They tied the cow to the back of the wagon. Annie dug some of her favorite bushes up by the roots and wrapped the ball of soil in moistened burlap and loaded them on the wagon. They drove the wagon the 35 miles from Walterboro to Beaufort. On the way they passed a house sporting a sign: "Fire wood for sale."

"Pull over there, Dowling," said Annie. "Maybe that fella will let our animals get a drink at his horse trough." Her motive for stopping, however, was not for water. She had an idea. "Having any luck selling firewood?" she asked, like some old curious woman.

"Little. Why? Y' wanna buy some?"

"Maybe. After we get settled. Do town folk come out here to buy?"

"Some, but it's a ways. Mos'ly folks goin' by."

"S'pose a coupla my boys wanted to buy a whole load. Could they get a good price?" asked Annie.

The old man considered her for a few moments. Then he said, "Tell ya what I'll do. I'll give it to them free. A free cord of wood for every cord they cut and split for me."

"Deal!" said Annie. "They'll be back tomorrow. Come on, Dowling. Let's get on to Beaufort."

The next spring Annie spoke at the Women's Missionary meeting at her church. She told the women at the meeting, "God sure works in funny ways. I thought God was punishing us for something when Edna caught our house on fire. I thought my life was ended. We'd spent thirty years building up that farm so we could buy it from Daddy. But we were too successful. Daddy wasn't eager to sell it. Every time we'd start talking about it, he'd raise the price. I'd ask why and he'd say it was worth more. If I said we made it worth more, he'd say if we didn't like it to move. Now he wants us to buy it and move back. But we have our own forty acres on Ladies Island. Dowling bought it from a man he works for just six months after we moved to Beaufort.

"My point is this. My daddy had us in a crunch. We couldn't buy and we didn't see how we could move. Then God took that accident by Edna to show us we could move. If we hadn't moved, my boys wouldn't have that wood yard.

If we hadn't moved, we wouldn't have that farm on Ladies Island. If we hadn't moved, I wouldn't be here with you. It was Edna that struck the matches, but God that made us move."

Lent 1
Romans 10:8b-13
By C. David McKirachan

Aren't You Ashamed?

I remember when everybody was Presbyterian. I was a kid. The church was a city of people, everybody going to Sunday school, choir, fellowship happenings, and worship. My father, the pastor, was a public figure, welcomed into the parlors and the chambers of the decision makers.

It isn't so now. It is kind of passe to be a Christian, especially if you aren't in a church with stadium seating and on television. We're not part of the social or political elite. We're received with great reservation by anyone who is a reasonable, intelligent, intellectual. I mean, who the hell believes all this stuff? Why don't we just stick to a humanistic agenda and stop messing around with all the old superstitious stories? Aren't they just so much antique sloppy thinking? Haven't we proven that the soul doesn't exist and love is little more than an enzyme?

So for us to proclaim Jesus Christ is Lord is a rather embarrassing social *faux pas* rather than a courageous announcement of faith.

Well, sorry to embarrass any of you who are reasonable and philosophically centered in a universe that needs no God, but I'm a dumb and old-fashioned cousin who comes from the backwater of Calvinism. In my silly retrograde stubbornness, I continue to preach a gospel that is not based on metaphor, but on the actual incarnation of a loving and personal spirit that infuses and sanctifies the universe.

I regret if this causes you to hem and haw a bit. I mean, I do periodically have interesting insights and I don't fit the profile of a Bible-thumping evangelist. But it's where I happen to stand in life and such is the truth. I will remind you that there is room at the table, the communion table that is. There is room there even for secular humanists. How could that be? Well, I'm not sure. If there is room for Jews and Greeks in the family of God, there might be room there for a few of you. I know you'd be slumming it. But you might give it a try. It's a fascinating anthropological phenomenon how these intelligent, educated, experienced people continue to believe in this Christianity business.

It may not be the center of social acceptance anymore. But it's still the way, the truth, and the life.

Thank you for your kind indulgence. Have a nice day.

Lent 2
Genesis 15:1-12, 17-18
by Scott Dalgarno

As Clear as the Milky Way

After these things the word of the LORD came to Abram in a vision, "Do not be afraid, Abram, I am your shield; your reward shall be very great." But Abram said, "O Lord GOD, what will you give me, for I continue childless, and the heir of my house is my cousin, Eliezer of Damascus?" — Genesis 15:1-2

Jay and Sarah found each other in college. Neither had dated much in high school. College represented a chance for both of them to get a new start and that was part of the bond that brought them together. They saw it in one another's eyes and in the geeky awkwardness each found attractive in the other.

They were engaged with astonishing speed, the way young people often are who find their first "true love." Their bond was strong. They felt as if they were meant for each other from before birth. Love was running away with them like a carriage without a driver. They decided they wanted four children. They even named them.

By their senior year, the "new" having worn off, both wondered if they had been emotionally hasty. Jay, in particular wondered what it would have been like had he tested the waters with several women before settling on one for life. They broke it off each assuring the other that they could always get back together if they wanted. The arrangement felt odd and reassuring at the same time.

Jay worked that summer at his father's restaurant in Seattle. He enjoyed his freedom but when September rolled around and, for the first time in his life, Jay found himself *not* going to school, he began to wonder if he had made a great mistake, breaking it off with Sarah. Taking the Labor Day weekend off, he made the three-hour drive hoping to surprise her, just showing up at her door.

He rang the bell with a giddy confidence but was a bit unnerved at her mother's initial unease at seeing him. Jay chalked it up to the breakup until she told him, haltingly, almost apologetically, that Sarah had been seeing someone else all summer and was once again, engaged.

Jay didn't have the heart to hang around another minute. He motored right home and did his best to move along in life. He applied to graduate schools all on the east coast thinking he needed a completely fresh start. Though he liked the fall colors in New England as much as anyone, he felt a certain culture shock, but when the next fall rolled around he dug into his studies and things went well enough for him to stick it out.

He more than welcomed the opportunity to go home for the holidays. It would be fun and his older brother was getting married right after Christmas. Jay would be a best man before he would be a groom. That felt somehow correct.

He found he thoroughly enjoyed planning a party for this brother. They had never been all that close before. On the big day Jay found himself listening very intently to everything the minister said during the ceremony. He saw himself right there, holding a woman's hands in his own.

He found the reception not to his taste, hating DJs and the obligatory playing of "Y-M-C-A" and "We Are Family," but he danced with a half dozen girls, asking Julie, his second cousin, to take several turns with him on the parquet floor. She seemed to enjoy the festive nature of it as much as he did. They managed to get together every day that vacation and, back at school, separated by 3,000 miles, they emailed often. Within weeks they found themselves talking about marriage, first, in general, then in reference to themselves.

It was odd, having a relationship develop that way, so far apart. There was something a bit unreal about it all, but Jay felt he wasn't getting any younger and he and Julie had quite a bit in common. With spring break coming, he bought her a ring and presented it to her at the family restaurant at an Easter morning brunch right in front of his family. Every one seemed so pleased for them both.

Later on that same morning he ran into his former fiancé Sarah's brother at church. He heard himself asking about Sarah. Was she well? Did she like being married? Dave, her brother, said that though she was still seeing Rick they hadn't married, and hadn't even set a date yet. Dave wrote down her number and presented it to Jay, encouraging him to call her. "She'd love hearing from you," he said.

Jay complied. He complied so quickly he called her from the narthex. He felt something break up inside himself at the word, "Hello." It was uncanny. It was like a spring thaw.

The two caught up quickly on the basics, but neither said anything to the other about their significant relationships. Then there was a long pause. How about coffee the next day, he said? Sarah related that she was leaving town to spend a week at the beach with her folks the next morning. She'd like to see him but it had to happen that afternoon. Jay said he had plans to do some shopping, but that it could probably wait a day, though he knew very well that he'd be on an airplane the next afternoon.

He thought about Sarah all the way through the service and was on his way to her house before the benediction was pronounced. Her mother answered the door once again, but this time she was chuckling.

Jay marveled at how easy it was catching up with Sarah. How it seemed they hadn't been apart a single day. They talked about everything — old friends, some of whom had already married and divorced. They talked about school, work, family, and pretty soon Sarah was crying and Jay found himself holding her in his arms. They talked the whole night.

It was near midnight when he finally asked her why she had gotten herself engaged again so quickly. "Oh," she said, "maybe it was because there wasn't a single thing about him that reminded me of you."

That night on the airplane, looking out at the stars, Jay felt shell-shocked. He was now promised to one woman and totally in love with another. He knew deep inside what he had to do. But what would he tell Julie? How would he break it to her?

Still, his heart was soaring now. His perspective was galactic. Why had he not seen this before? Any time he'd put himself in charge of engineering his own happiness, he'd made a mess of it. Life was so much bigger than he was, he thought. Everything of real worth was a gift, not contrived. It was as clear as the Milky Way.

Lent 3
Isaiah 55:1-9
by Rick McCracken-Bennett

God's Dinner Bell

> *Ho, everyone who thirsts, come to the waters; and you that have no money, come, buy and eat! Come, buy wine and milk without money and without price. Why do you spend your money for that which is not bread, and your labor for that which does not satisfy? Listen carefully to me, and eat what is good, and delight yourselves in rich food.* — Isaiah 55:1-2

Growing up, I always thought we should have had a dinner bell. My friend Jim, who lived on another farm a mile or so away — less if you trekked through the woods, through the swamp (what we now more elegantly call a wetland), across his dad's fields, and up his lane to his house — *he* had a dinner bell. The bell was gold-colored, probably brass. There was a rope that hung from some sort of rocker deal on top of the bell. It was mounted on a post, right near the side door that led to the kitchen, and if you were in the kitchen, you could go out the door and walk a few steps to the summer kitchen, where it was a lot cooler to cook on those hot summer days.

In the summer we would play together almost every day. And just before noon, if it had already been cleared with my mother, the dinner bell would ring and we would race to the house to clean up and sit down to a real farmer's meal, complete with all the foods that most of us banned from our diets years ago. She didn't have to ring twice. She didn't have to say, "Stop your fooling around and get your fannies in here." She just had to give it a ring and we would take off running, brushing the dirt off of our jeans in puffs like smoke, salivating like a couple of Pavlov's dogs.

After a prayer, we would stuff ourselves and drink gallons of sweetened ice tea (which, for reasons that are lost in my childhood memory bank, we called "bug juice"). There was always enough food. Actually, there was always more than enough. If I brought my little brother along, there was enough. If we invited Steve up the road and Randy rode his bike over, there was enough. "Come and get it," the bell would say. "Eat up!" it rang. And we would eat and talk and laugh and tell stories. I remember feeling that I was just about the luckiest kid around, to have such good friends, and to have such wonderful food to eat.

We were always allowed to play in their barn. But one thing was off limits. It was a rope — a big, thick, rough rope that hung from one of the rafters and had a huge knot on the end. His folks would warn us to never, ever swing from that rope. It was too dangerous. But, of course, we did swing from it… every day we played together. One afternoon it was my turn to swing out of the hayloft and down to the floor. Apparently I grabbed the rope at a lower place than usual and like a modern-day bungee jumper who miscalculated the distance to the ground, I hit the floor and the momentum dragged me several more feet, pulling my shin over the head of a nail that was sticking out of the floor. I still have the scar. We were afraid to tell his mom, but what could we do? My jeans were ripped and bloodied. As expected, Jim's mother hit the roof — just like my mom would do later. Jim's mother cleaned up my wound, poured on something that both stung and stained, and after applying the bandage, sent us out to the porch to sit and not say a word while she called my mom to come and get me. I don't know if the wound or the scolding hurt more.

I didn't return to Jim's for a couple of days. It was probably my punishment. And when I was finally allowed to go over I thought that things would be different, that his parents wouldn't treat me the same, that there would be more and stricter rules. But as I climbed their front steps his mother greeted me with an ice-cold glass of sweetened bug juice. She said that she expected me to stay for dinner. And it was all like before, except that now I knew what it meant to have done something wrong, receive the punishment I deserved, and then be welcomed back to the banquet. And what a wonderful feeling it was!

Lent 4
2 Corinthians 5:16-21
by David O. Bales

The Ugliest Man in the World

All spring of 1939, Flora had tried to get her daughter Aida to attend Sunday school at the American church. But Paris was always more interesting. Aida, the only American in the *lycée*, seemed to be invited to every event on every weekend by every other student. Besides, after finally agreeing to attend Sunday school, Aida found that the teacher spoke English poorly. "I think Monsieur Sordet teaches the class so he can practice his English. I can hardly understand him. The three Brits in class just turn their heads and laugh. And really," Aida sniffed as she tapped her index finger on her mother's wrist, "Monsieur Sordet is the ugliest man in the world."

Besides trying to get Aida to Sunday school at the American church, Flora had all she could manage as a single mother and bread-winner. Her job at the U.S. embassy was already overwhelming. Embassy desks were stacked high with requests for visas from Spanish refugees. Flora would say, "America just isn't granting visas to Spaniards. But I'll phone the Mexican embassy and tell them I'm sending you over." Now, along with the Spaniards who'd escaped to France during the Spanish Civil War, refugees poured into Paris from Germany. The embassy staff called them "Hitler's flotsam and jetsam": German intellectuals and Jews. Many of them resembled Flora's grandparents. Some resembled Flora herself.

With the added stress of trying to save lives, Flora remained faithful to weekly worship and called upon her faith as she'd never considered possible. She prayed almost constantly during working hours as people waited in line to see her. They stood outside the embassy, lining up around the block. The same people returned every week, asking and then begging for a visa to America — and becoming thinner and more threadbare.

Flora and Aida's lives hung by the thinnest financial thread. Three years earlier Flora and Skip had received the telegram accepting his proposal for study at the Louvre. They didn't know and couldn't predict that his weak aortic artery would burst, leaving him dead in less than a minute and leaving Flora and Aida stranded in France without a job or support. Flora had struggled through grief and poverty at the same time, and she believed that her prayers were answered when she got the job at the embassy.

Aida's time was consumed by her high school chums. Flora's energy was daily sapped by inspecting outdated or obviously forged passports and saying, "I'm sorry. There're just no visas for the U.S."

Flora continued to pray until praying wasn't an act of will but of her nature. Only occasionally did Flora get Aida to Sunday school, and she'd come home with some complaint about Monsieur Sordet. "Mom, when he tries to read through those thick glasses, he looks like he's peering through a couple of portholes."

Their frayed existence began thoroughly to unravel when Hitler shattered the precarious phony war in May 1940. France formally surrendered on June 22. Although they were U.S. citizens, Flora's having Jewish grandparents placed them in instant jeopardy. She'd seen and heard enough from German refugees not to wait for Nazi troops to march into Paris.

Two days before the Germans occupied Paris, neighbors offered her and Aida a place in a car fleeing south. In twelve minutes they'd stuffed a suitcase apiece. In what was soon to become Vichy France, the port of Marseille beckoned as an open door out of a house fire.

On their second day, the car ran out of gas and no one would sell them more. Amid the scuffling and shoving of other refugees, they became separated from their neighbors when they entered a village. Within two kilometers beyond the village they were robbed of everything — including passports and visas.

Now only their physical strength could get them to safety. Flora and Aida walked every day. A few villagers gave them a little to eat. More often, low on food for themselves and low on patience with strangers, they warned refugees to keep moving.

Two weeks later and fifteen pounds lighter they arrived in Marseille and learned that two groups were helping refugees. They leaped at the hope. As they walked into the small hotel room to meet the Assistance Committee, a voice in broken English greeted them: "Ah, Aida. I'm so glad to see you." Hugs and tears followed between Aida, Flora, and Monsieur Sordet.

After a week's hiding and preparing, they were instructed to arrive at exactly 6 a.m. at a particular ship on the waterfront. Monsieur Sordet rushed up to them. He handed them passports and visas and hustled them onto the ship. The gangplank pulled up behind them and the ship immediately began to move. They had a moment to wave to Monsieur Sordet. He looked up at them through his giant glasses and waved back, then walked away quickly. They were on their way to the Caribbean island of Martinique and from there to the United States.

Flora and Aida stood with an arm around each other, watching their beloved France recede. For the first time in weeks they both breathed normally. Flora was still praying. She said to Aida, "Now what do you think of Monsieur Sordet?"

Aida tugged a little on her mother, rocking her slightly. She said, "I think he's about the handsomest man in the world."

Lent 5
Psalm 126
by Sandra Herrmann

Panic and Recovery

Many of us have experienced the total panic that ensues when we discover that our wallet has been lost — or, God forbid, stolen. We frantically search our various pockets or purses. We check the bedroom — maybe when I undressed yesterday I dropped it? Maybe it fell off the dresser or table? Well, before moving furniture I'll go out and look in the car. It would be easy enough for it to fall out as I got into the car or out of it.

Once out at the car, we have to check under the seats. If your wallet is thinner than mine, you'll run your hand between the seat and the back. Check the backseat too, because if it fell out in the car it could have slid through to the backseat. Be sure to run your hand as far under as you can reach.

Well, this is distressing. If it's not in the car and it wasn't where it should have been in the house, where could it be? Now it's time to sit down, breathe a little, and think. Where do you last remember seeing it?

The last time I had this experience, I had been at church. I remembered taking it out of my pocket/purse to pay for supper. At the time I was concerned because I thought I had taken the money I got at the ATM and put it in my wallet, but the cash wasn't there. I had to write a check. I checked my purse again and found the checkbook still in my purse.

I had stopped to get gas after that. Did I have my wallet then? I realized that I wasn't sure if I had the wallet, because I had discovered the ATM money in my coat pocket. But I hadn't reached for my wallet at the time — I just paid with cash.

Oh dear. Well, time to call the gas station. Was my wallet turned in? No? Are you *sure*? Okay, thanks.

Called church. Was a wallet like mine turned in to the secretary? Did the pastor see it by chance? No. But the secretary will pray for me to find it. That's nice of her. Maybe that will even work.

I went back to the bedroom and tracked my movements of the night before as best I could. Oh Lord, help me find that wallet. One good thing: I know there wasn't cash in it. Just my credit cards, driver's license, blood bank card, two gift cards I haven't used yet, insurance cards, my ID for the Y, my MedicAlert© card with half my life's information, my ATM card. (Oh, I'd better check my pockets! Do I remember putting it back in my wallet or is it with the cash in my pocket?) It's in the wallet. Well, at least no one can get my money without the PIN.

The more I think about how bad this whole thing is, the less sure I am of anything. And I'm starting to worry about contacting all those companies to get my cards stopped, just in case it was stolen. I'm starting to pace, worrying, looking in places I've already looked just in case.

So I hopped in the car and drove only slightly above the speed limit to get to the church so I could search there. It's not in the coat area. Not under the couch where I'd sat and talked with a friend. If it had been under any of the tables or chairs, someone would have taken it to the secretary's office, or even called me, because I had accurate identification in there.

Then I realize — I went into the sound room to talk to the techs about getting a CD of the Sunday service. I'd sat down for a minute while they got out the CD and put it in a case. Could the wallet be in there? Last chance. If it's not here, it's really gone, and maybe stolen. From the church, of all places. But when I bent over and looked, there it was, hiding under a chair in the sound room. Whew!

I went back to the secretary's office and said, "Rejoice with me, for the lost is found!" And she did. I laughed, and we talked about the panic that ensues when you can't find your wallet or your keys. I'm babbling about this event. I realize that I'm positively giddy.

Since I've never been a refugee, never been torn from my home and family and carried away to a foreign land against my will, I will never know how those returning from Babylon felt. But in the words of this Psalm and my words: "You restored my fortune, O Lord, and I, who was terrified, have reaped with a song of joy. Thank you, God, for helping me find my life again."

I sang hymns of praise all the way back home.

Passion / Palm Sunday
Luke 22:14—23:56
by Peter Andrew Smith

Passionate Sense

Suzanne began straightening hymnbooks and picking up leftover bulletins as soon people started leaving the church. Somehow worship didn't seem complete for her unless everything was ready for the next service. After a few minutes, the only one left in the church was a young man sitting in the back with his head bowed.

"Sorry," he said as she worked her way over to him. "I guess I should be leaving."

Suzanne motioned for him to remain. "You stay as long as you like. No one should ever be rushed out of church."

"Thanks," he said with a slight smile, and he bowed his head again.

She continued her trek through the pews but snuck an occasional glance his way. She thought the young man looked familiar, but she couldn't remember if he usually came by himself or with someone else.

Suzanne reached the final pew and deposited the collected papers in the recycling bin. She made sure the other doors were locked and went back into the sanctuary. The young man was still deep in thought. She quietly walked down the side aisle and slipped into the seat beside him.

He saw her and smiled again. "I suppose you need me to go so you can lock up."

"I'm not in a hurry to go anywhere," she said, extending her hand. "I've seen you here before, but I can't put a name to you. My name is Suzanne."

"Chuck," he said, shaking her hand. "I work at the hospital in the labs."

"Pleased to meet you," she said. "You still thinking about this morning's service?"

"I am. Hearing the story of Jesus all the way from the Last Supper to the cross is pretty intense."

"It sure is," Suzanne said. "Every time I hear it I discover something new."

"Really?"

"Sure. This morning I was struck by how no one knew what to do with Jesus. After he was arrested they kept sending him here and there before Pilate finally condemned him. They seemed confused as to what to do with him."

"Huh," Chuck said. "I can understand that, because I'm not sure what to do with Jesus either."

"What do you mean?"

"Well," he said, "there seems to be so much in the story — his breaking bread with the disciples, his time in the garden, his trial, and his death on the cross. I'm not sure what all of it means." He looked into her face. "Why did Jesus die?"

"That's a good question, and I think the pastor could probably answer that one better than me," Suzanne said. "But I know it's because Jesus loves us and wanted to save us from sin and death."

"I've heard that explanation before, but I can't understand it up here," he said, pointing to his head.

"Hmm, I'm not sure that love ever makes sense up there." Suzanne rubbed her chin for a moment. "You got a wife or a girlfriend?"

"Yeah."

"You understand in your head why she loves you?"

"No," Chuck said with a smile. "Sometimes for the life of me I don't know why she does."

"But when she does something loving," Suzanne said, pointing to his chest, "you know it in there, don't you?"

"I sure do."

"I think that's why they call those parts of the gospel the Passion. We're meant to feel them in our hearts even when we can't sort them out in our heads."

"But how can I feel it in my heart?" he asked.

"Well, I use this time of year to walk with Jesus through the story."

"But it's Jesus' story, not mine."

Suzanne shook her head. "No, Chuck. I know that Jesus means the story to be ours too because he kept people with him the whole way — and asks us to be there too."

"What do you mean?"

"Who was in the upper room?"

"The disciples," Chuck answered, "but wasn't Jesus alone in the garden when he prayed?"

"Naw, there were disciples with him, although they kept falling asleep. And they were there when he got arrested."

"Ah, Suzanne, but then they all ran away."

"Yeah, most of them might have, but remember that Peter followed. And I bet some of those fellows around when Jesus went on trial were followers, even if they didn't dare say it."

"But Jesus was alone after he was condemned."

"No, there were disciples around him then as well. They may have been at a distance and horrified by what they saw, but they were there to watch Jesus die."

Chuck thought about it for a while. "So you think that by hearing those stories and thinking about being there I'll understand them?"

"I'm not sure," Suzanne said, "but you'll experience them, and I think that is why the gospel writers wrote them for us."

Chuck looked at her for a few minutes and took her hand. "Thank you."

"Always a pleasure," Suzanne said. "And don't forget that the Passion isn't the only thing to experience this time of year."

Chuck tilted his head to one side. "What do you mean?"

"The journey to the cross isn't finished until we reach Easter morning," Suzanne said. "See you next Sunday?"

"I'll be here," Chuck said.

Suzanne followed him out the door as she knew that everything was finally ready for the next time of worship.

Maundy Thursday
1 Corinthians 11:23-26
by Frank Ramirez

Julia Gilbert Changes Love Feast Among the Brethren — Twice!

For I received from the Lord what I also handed on to you...
— 1 Corinthians 11:23a

The venerable elders of the old Dunkers, one of the German Plain People sometimes referred to as the Pennsylvania Dutch, would meet yearly to argue their arcane understanding of the scriptures in order to be true in their faith and practice. What they received from their reading of the Lord's word they assiduously handed on to the next generation. They changed, if at all, very slowly. Though in theory anyone could speak at their Annual Meetings, in practice the respect accorded to their elders, with their long beards and plain garb, meant that they had a greater voice.

Nowhere were traditions more honored than in the long and complex ritual known as the Love Feast. This communion service, often stretching over three days, included a foot-washing ceremony and an agape meal, along with the bread and cup. This was their signature practice, which others found so intriguing that many would come to witness the celebration.

So it is all the more surprising that these traditions were changed — twice — by a woman who was disabled, once when she was a teenager, and once decades later after a lifelong struggle.

Julia Gilbert (1844-1934) was born near the foot of South Mountain in Frederick County, Maryland, but when she was four her family moved to Wolfe Creek in western Ohio. She attended her first Annual Meeting at the age of six and rarely missed another through her long life.

When she was eight years old, two of her siblings died when they contracted measles and scarlet fever. She barely survived herself and was crippled for life.

In 1858, at the age of fourteen, she was baptized in the rushing stream. At first she was reluctant to step into the water in her fragile condition, afraid of being swept away, but her pastor reminded her that Jesus had been there before. Recalling the baptism of Jesus by John the Baptist, she stepped out into the river and as she knelt she prayed, "Dear God, I promise to you that I will live faithful to Jesus until I die." She kept that promise.

She eagerly looked forward to the Love Feast that was celebrated following her baptism as a meal she was sharing with Jesus. The experience was joyful but that night she found she could not sleep, and she finally lit a candle and read John 13:4: "He riseth from supper, and laid aside his garments; and took a towel, and girded himself."

The next day she asked her father why the Wolfe Creek congregation had performed the foot washing and then set the meal on the table. Shouldn't they have set the meal on the table and then, like Jesus, risen from the table for the foot washing? Her father, according to her report, sighed and answered, "The old Brethren took the ordinance from several passages of scripture and thought this to be the proper way it ought to be done." This satisfied her for a day or two but eventually she questioned the elders, and the next year the congregation changed the way they performed Love Feast to conform to the fourteen-year-old's reading of scripture.

By contrast, her next cause took nearly fifty years before it was successfully concluded. In her day, men passed a long strip of communion bread to each other, each breaking off a piece, but the women did not break bread with each other.

Instead, an elder walked down the row and the sisters broke off a piece. This did not seem biblical to Julia, nor was she satisfied with the official explanations for the practice. For decades, first in Ohio and later in Iowa, where she moved after her parents' deaths, she championed the cause, only to see it tabled or returned at Annual Meetings. Finally in June of 1910, at Winona Lake, Indiana, Julia herself spoke on the floor of Annual Meeting, saying, "When I was baptized, I made a vow to God to walk in all his ways and to read the scriptures. I believe it is our duty to do things the way Jesus taught us to do them." The motion passed and the next year the sisters broke the bread among themselves.

Paul wrote his exhortation to the Corinthians not to preserve some imagined purity of practice — what he had passed on was the practice of coming together at the table to commemorate the Passion of Jesus Christ. A reading of the larger context of the text makes it clear that the real problem in Corinth was that not all were sharing equally around the table. Rich were arriving early and eating all the good food of the agape meal, leaving the poor, who worked, to eat later and less. Regardless of the century in which we live, Jesus calls us as equals to his table, prepared to listen and learn from each other, and to recognize that the Spirit dwells richly among us all.

Good Friday
John 18:1—19:42
by Rick McCracken-Bennett

Betrayal in the Third Grade

> So Judas brought a detachment of soldiers together with police from the chief priests and the Pharisees, and they came there with lanterns and torches and weapons. Then Jesus, knowing all that was to happen to him, came forward and asked them, "Whom are you looking for?" They answered, "Jesus of Nazareth." Jesus replied, "I am he." Judas, who betrayed him, was standing with them. — John 18:3-5

> One of the slaves of the high priest, a relative of the man whose ear Peter had cut off, asked, "Did I not see you in the garden with him?" Again Peter denied it, and at that moment the cock crowed. — John 18:26-27

(Kids say the darnedest things... sometimes, like adults, they say the most awful things.)

You would be inclined to give them a break. After all, they were only third-grade boys.

You would say, "They were too young to have known what they were doing," or "Knowing right from wrong, especially in this case, would be too difficult for nine- and ten-year-old boys to comprehend." And you would be right, and... you would be wrong.

It was fall; a new school year had just barely gotten underway. Even for the Midwest, it was warm, too warm to sit in a stuffy, old classroom with freshly varnished floors that reflected the room in swirly, uneven patterns. Recess, as always, was a welcome relief. This particular day they were going to get a little extra time on the playground. There was to be a softball game and everyone was invited to join in. All morning long the room was buzzing with third-grade wonderings about who among them co-captains Don and Randy, the best players in the whole elementary school, would pick for their team.

Recess didn't start when the first bell rang. The students stared at their teacher and then at each other, and she just sat sadly at her desk. Every minute or so she would pull open her middle desk drawer and rummage around a little before closing it and looking out at her class. Something was up and none of the kids knew what it was. They just sat there casting sideways glances at each other.

Finally Mrs. Watkins stood up, slid her chair in, cleared her throat, looked the class over, and spoke slowly and carefully. "I'm not sure how to say this, boys and girls. Someone has been in my desk and has stolen the milk money for this afternoon's snack." She paused, quickly swiped an eye with her fingers, and went on. "This is serious, because it means that one of us cannot be trusted. Someone here is a thief. And I suspect that some of you know who did this. So… we will not go out to recess, and we will not have our softball game; in fact, we will not have any recess until the person who took this money comes forward. I am so disappointed, boys and girls. I hope we can take care of this quickly."

The room went into shock. Not so much that the money had been stolen — few of the kids hadn't made off with a little change from their mother's purse from time to time — but rather because the softball game of the century and their chance to whip the fourth graders was being canceled. Stunned, the children sat there, and when Mrs. Watkins wasn't looking, snuck a glance with raised eyebrows and got shrugs from each other which said, "I don't know what to do either."

The second bell for recess rang out in the hallway.

An eternity passed when a crumpled-up note landed on Steve Richards' desk. Slowly, with his eyes steadily on his teacher, he unfolded the note. His eyes grew wide as he read, "Let's tell her that Robbie did it." Robbie wasn't a friend. In fact, few kids in the class liked him at all. Steve shot a glance at Randy, who nodded almost imperceptibly back at him, and then at Don — and there you had it, three third-grade co-conspirators. A couple more notes passed and they were ready with their plan.

As the third bell rang, telling the older kids to line up for recess, they stood, and with a nod to each other, Steve, Randy, and Don approached their teacher. Their guilty looks probably made Mrs. Watkins think that they were the guilty party. "Mrs. Watkins?" Randy took the lead. "Mrs. Watkins, we know who took the money."

"Yes?" she replied, looking dead into his eyes but with her face cocked to one side. "Who, then? Who did this?"

Randy looked at Steve and then at Don and then blurted out in a stage whisper, "Robbie… Robbie did it. Now, can we go to recess?"

"Go back to your seats," Mrs. Watkins said softly. "Everyone… may I have your attention?" Which wasn't necessary since everyone's eyes were fixed at first on the boys, and now on her. "I want you to line up for recess. Robbie… I would like you to remain here with me."

The class lined up and then made their way to the playground. But there was no softball that day. Randy and Don didn't pick teams. They and Steve Richards just stood together, unable to look each other in the eye. When the bell rang for them to return, they walked silently to the luke-warm drinking fountain and then to their classroom. Everyone sat down.

"Class? Robbie will not be with us for the next two days. He has been suspended for taking the milk money from my desk. When he returns I expect you to treat him in the same way that you would like to be treated if the shoe were on the other foot. Do you all understand?" The class nodded as one.

On the bus that afternoon, Randy and Steve and Don sat together in the back. "Now what are we going to do? What should we do? Should we tell Mrs. Watkins?" But the question that they couldn't quite answer, because after all they were just third-grade boys, was why he accepted his punishment when he was innocent? Why didn't he speak up? Why didn't he tell on them, for it was obvious who lied about him? And even though they didn't understand the deeper questions at the time, they thought often as they grew up about the sacrifice Robbie made that hot fall day.

It may be just a coincidence — yeah, that's probably it, just a coincidence — that Robbie became a minister out of college and is still to this day.

Easter Day
Acts 10:34-43
by Stan Purdum

Eyewitnesses

> *...but God raised him on the third day and allowed him to appear, not to all the people but to us who were chosen by God as witnesses...* — Acts 10:40-41a

"It couldn't have been him," the distraught woman said. "I talked to him not more than an hour ago."

The police officer shifted uneasily on his feet. These things were never easy. "I'm so sorry, ma'am," he said, "but we identified him from his driver's license. And the car was registered in his name as well."

"Well, it's got to be a mistake. It's not him."

"Actually," replied the officer, "we will need someone to formally identify him."

"I'll do it." That was from the woman's sixteen-year-old son, Ryan. She didn't know how long he had been standing behind her but suddenly she was glad he was there. He was such a level-headed boy. He'd be able to straighten out this colossal mistake. One look and he'd know the man lying in morgue was not his father. And then the police could put their energies into finding out who the unfortunate driver was.

"Thank you, Ryan," she said. Then, turning to the officer, she added, "My son will go with you, and you'll see. It's not my Tom you've got there." The starch in her voice was almost convincing but both the officer and Ryan noticed the quiver in her lip.

"Is there someone we can call for you first?" the officer asked.

"Not necessary," the woman said, gathering her courage. "You'll have Ryan back in no time. You'll see."

It was less than an hour later when Ryan came back. But as he opened the door, his mother took one look at him and knew the awful truth.

They crumpled into each other's arms, sobbing with great grief.

* * *

"It couldn't have been him," Philip said. "They crucified him. All Jerusalem saw it. Nobody could have survived that. He's dead. I didn't want to believe it, but it's true."

Mary Magdalene could hardly stand still, even though she'd run all the way from the tomb. "But it was him," she said, "He spoke to me."

"You've got to be mistaken, woman. It's not him."

"Actually," replied Mary, "John and Peter have been to the tomb. It's empty."

"Yes, they told me. But all that proves is that his body has been moved."

Mary realized that Philip was not going to be convinced by anything she said, so finally she simply told him, "You just wait. You'll see."

Much later that day, she entered the house where the Eleven had been staying. Except for Thomas, they were all there.

And all ten of them were sobbing with great joy.

Easter 2
Acts 5:27-32
by John S. Smylie

We Must Obey God

We must obey God rather than any human authority.
— Acts 5:29b

He was only nineteen years old, more than a little idealistic and was about to engage in a spiritual journey that would last for a lifetime. After partying deep into the late hours of the night he resented the loud alarm clock demanding his attention, screaming out to him that it was time to get up, time to get out of bed and go to his sociology class. He had no idea that this day would be a day that would influence the rest of his life. After throwing water on his face and brushing his teeth, hoping to camouflage the scent of the previous night, he descended on the elevator from the top floor of his high-rise dorm room and faced the chilly air — and the steps that seem to be designed for dogs rather than human beings… annoying steps, one step up then another step to reach the next step up, thereby always having to use the same leg for the up step.

He reached his sociology class that met at the University Chapel, a space that could accommodate the over 800 students that gathered twice a week. This was a lousy learning environment, made even worse by a lack of sleep and a professor whose lecture might as well have been read from the assigned textbook. After class he walked down the dog steps and into the foyer of the dormitory, pushed the up button for the elevator, stepped inside, pushed 20, and ascended to the top floor. Throwing his books on his desk, he pulled the curtains shut and climbed back into bed. He fell asleep within a few minutes and had a dream that changed his life.

The dream was simple... he was given an image of himself as God saw him — an image that was very different than the one he had formed of himself. The dream offered him a vision of his life first as a young man, then as an old man. He was dressed in light, able to give and receive love, and he knew that he was glimpsing his truest self. Upon awakening he discovered that his mind had been branded by the powerful image that he knew was impressed upon him by God almighty. From that moment on he began to seek God's light.

When our lives are touched by the reality of the holy, we continue to have choices — yet our choices become narrower and at times more obvious. It seems that our choices are really quite simple: we either choose to obey God or we are miserable. The young man in this story would soon discover that he had to make a choice whether to follow the prompting of the Holy Spirit or to follow the wishes of his parents. He announced to his parents that he was leaving college to pursue a spiritual journey. His parents thought he was crazy and expressed their concerns in no uncertain terms; they didn't understand or support his decision to leave college. He needed to discover more about the power of God, while his parents understood that he needed an education to be successful in the world. But the Spirit was calling him to a different knowledge: "We must obey God rather than any human authority." He left college, returning later to complete his education after experiencing a journey that taught him about faith and holiness. That journey is another story too long to tell here.

Years later he found himself at a divinity school, preparing to serve as a minister, when the Spirit again called him to leave the seminary environment and also to sell everything that he had and give it to the poor. This time his mother nearly had a heart attack at the thought of him giving away the inheritance that he had received from her father, his grandfather. "We must obey God rather than any human authority."

He did leave the seminary, and he did sell everything he had and gave it to the poor — and to his surprise he was invited to live in a monastic community where he experienced daily worship, contemplative prayer, and the deep healing power of our Lord Jesus Christ. His journey continues to this day. As he listens for the wind of the Spirit and the call of Jesus, he continues to find himself in unexpected adventures with the choice of obedience to God always before him.

As we look at our lives, we may ask: What risk is the Spirit calling us to take? As we think of what God is doing in our faith communities, in our families, and in our personal lives, it may be good for us to ask ourselves if our faith communities, our families, and our personal lives show obedience to God rather than to human authorities, or even worse, to self-centered and sinful desires. A true journey of faith will likely take us to places that we never dreamed we would go, and yet we can be sure that we will be blessed and God will be honored if we choose to obey our Lord's will and live out his vision for each of us.

We can imagine those first apostles filled with the Spirit of God, filled with confidence and courage, filled with the desire to share the good news of the life-giving power over sin and death that they found in connecting their lives with the living God through the person of Jesus Christ. May our choices reflect the same obedience to God and may our lives show forth his presence in our communities, in our families, and in ourselves. Let us obey God rather than any human authority!

Easter 3
Acts 9:1-6 (7-20)
by Scott Dalgarno

The Good Little Girl

Kathleen had always been the good little girl and it had nearly killed her. As a child she found that whatever she did to please her mother, it usually made her father mad. And it went the other way too. She was an only child and her father wanted a son, so he did his utmost to make her into what pleased him. He took her shooting with him. He made her play baseball. She was no athlete, but she did her best — and her best at baseball and target practice always left her mother cold. When her mother would dress her in gingham, her father looked as if she were a total disappointment. Poor Kathleen didn't know what to do. But instead of complaining she did her best to comply with everyone. And it nearly made her sick.

Her frustration at the impossible task of pleasing everyone wasn't enough to sink her. No, she managed to marry (twice, in fact), have three children, finish her M.B.A., and take care of the everyday operations of a medium-sized bank for years. And every day she ran a gauntlet at home and work — because there is no way anyone on this planet can keep everybody within shouting distance smiling.

Still, she tried. There was the divorce and a remarriage, and still she set her sights on being the most compliant, most attractive, most nurturing wife and mother in the world. At work she put in sixty hours a week trying to keep everyone above and below her in a state of peace and productivity. She was good at it.

She had been a person of faith since childhood. Her mother's mother had seen to that, much to the chagrin of her father who wanted his daughter to be completely self-reliant, like he was. "What Would Jesus Do?" was her motto; she thought of her home and office as her ministry and viewed everyone around her as disciples who she felt she needed to keep clean and fed and on track.

"Give me strength, God" was her prayer every day — and God seemed to give it to her every morning... until she was about forty. That's when the wheels started to come loose from the great enterprise of her life.

The bank, locally owned for the first ten years she worked at it, had been bought by a large conglomerate. New policy statements were sent to her by the dozen. Every day there were fresh complaints from the troops and who did they come to? Kathleen, of course. She handled them as well as she could to begin with but in a matter of months her resolve began to crumble. She'd wake at two in the morning night after night trying to find a way through the mess. But she felt like the Dutch boy who put his fingers in the dike — new holes kept springing up.

When her husband Rick began complaining that things at home were not as they'd been and their two children, Becca and Brandi, began acting out all over the place, Kathleen knew a reckoning was coming.

Still, she forged ahead with superglue and duct tape until the Easter afternoon of her 41st year. The neighborhood was always invited to Kathleen and Rick's for brunch after church on Easter. And in they came — a score of them, with kids in tow. The smell of ham filled the house but there had been a glitch. Kathleen's famous twice-baked potatoes were a total loss — something about the sour cream being "off." Maybe it was that alone or maybe it was the fight she'd had with Rick that morning before church about him playing golf instead of helping with setting up, or the fact that Becca's retainer was lost for the hundredth time — whatever, Kathleen, for the first time in her life, melted down.

She'd lost her temper before, of course. But this time there was a definite break going on. She walked right past Mary Patterson, ignoring completely her apology for bringing her cousin Ginny without calling ahead. With the house full she retreated upstairs to her office and sat herself down in her late grandmother's overstuffed chair, where she began to let herself come unglued.

A size seven, she suddenly felt heavy, pressed down by the weight of what she felt was an entire life of failure. She felt a failure as a mother, a failure as a wife twice, a failure as a manager, a homemaker, a daughter. Suddenly all the things she had ever accomplished meant nothing to her and all the things she had wanted to do were like so much trash.

Right there, on that Easter afternoon with a houseful of guests, Kathleen unloaded completely on God. She told God that she had done her best to be a good mother and wife, a fine employee, a caring daughter and aunt and neighbor — and it all amounted to nothing. She was tired of trying. More than that, she was done with it. She no longer cared if the neighbors felt welcome in her home, no longer cared if her daughter's teeth were straight. It meant nothing to her that her husband loved her or that her son would pass the A.P. class she had tutored him in. She didn't care if her mother ever called, or if her boss praised her or fired her. She was exhausted in a way she had never known, and she was not at all interested in pleasing another human being for the rest of her life.

What surprised her was that she didn't feel the least bit guilty for her feelings, nor did she feel glad. In fact, she realized that she didn't feel anything at all. There, with the April sun streaming in on her from the skylight, she heard a line from Saint Therese uttered in her grandmother's voice — something she'd heard a hundred times but not for a dozen years — "If you can serenely bear the trial of being displeasing to yourself, you will be for Jesus a pleasant place of shelter."

Now, for the first time in her life, she took these words to heart. She knew that they were absolutely true and true for her. And in the stillness of that moment with the murmur of Easter company below her, she began to breathe deeply and easily, and she also began to heal.

Easter 4
John 10:22-30
by C. David McKirachan

Who Do You Trust?

Jesus wasn't a shepherd... and neither am I — but I'm pretty clear on this business of people who aren't part of the bunch not getting it. It's difficult at best to communicate the firm realities of salvation and hope to people who live in the darkness of a universe built on the hard realities of power and privilege, or measurable and attainable, or practical and profitable, or America and family, or any of the other normalities of our culture's mythological structure. "Tell us clearly whether or not you are the Christ." Such a demand is so weird that it boggles the mind. What did he need to do? What did they want? What proof would create the gravity that could break the hold of their expectation and judgment?

When I was ten, my older sister and I journeyed with my parents to the country estate of Miss Anne, one of the pillars of my father's church. "Rose Garden" (as it was known) was a working farm, animals and all. We were gussied up, so we had to be careful where we stepped and what we did. A pasture stretched out from a gate with stone posts. Out under trees on its far side, a small flock of sheep grazed. I was fascinated with them, and so my indulgent sister helped me over the gate and watched me journey toward the sheep, a bunch of green grass clutched in my hand as a peace offering and an incentive for them to trust me.

They bunched together, one of them (larger than the rest) making noises that sounded anxious. I kept on. Finally the big guy came toward me. I was encouraged and held out the offering. I remember wondering what one should say to a sheep. "Nice sheep" seemed lame, so I kept my silence and let the grass do the talking.

To make a long story short, the ram (which I'm sure he was) came close, reared up on his hind legs, and butted me in the middle. The only reason I didn't fall in the mud was because he stepped on my foot and I grabbed his head. At that point I took off running, with him in hot pursuit. My sister had climbed over the fence, laughing so hard she couldn't speak. So much for gentle sheep.

The basic problem was that I wasn't on the ram's list — I was a stranger. It wouldn't have mattered if I had some sheep candy and a bribe for the big guy. It wouldn't have mattered if I knew what to say. He was having none of it and none of me.

So maybe what they thought of Jesus' teaching and what they subsequently did to him is understandable. But *we aren't sheep!* We have choices to make that can bring us to new worlds of hope and abundant life. You'd think we'd learn. Maybe we're not hungry enough. Like those fat woolies on Miss Anne's farm, we're too well fed. We're not desperate enough to listen to a new voice. We want more proof. Oh well, missed the Lord again.

I wonder what was going through the ram's head when he chased me across the pasture. I wonder if he thought he won. My sister never told anybody about that day. She's cool.

Easter 5
Revelation 21:1-6
by Rick McCracken-Bennett

Everything Old Is New Again

See, I am making all things new.
— Revelation 21:5a

In Revelation (and other places in scripture) we're told that God is in the business of making all things new. What does that mean when the thing God is making new is us?

Years ago my baby sister wandered into a store — a junk store, really. She walked up and down the cluttered aisles not looking for anything in particular. She was just about ready to leave when a piece caught her eye. It was a bookstand — dusty, dirty, covered with (she found out soon enough) five layers of paint over the original varnish. "How much do you want for this?" was answered with "How much would you give?" and a few minutes and a little good-natured haggling later Kay walked out with her purchase.

She wasn't immediately struck with buyer's remorse; it was more like buyer's confusion. What was she going to do with it? How could she restore it? She had no idea.

Kay asked around at work and finally contacted a furniture refinisher. He gave her some ideas about what kind of noxious chemicals would remove the layers of paint. He told her a little about sanding and refinishing, and then he said, "But the most important thing is love. You've got to love the piece… see beyond the scratches and the paint and the dirt. You need to spend time with it, love it, and see it as it can be, not as it is."

So Kay spent time with it: holding it, looking at it, examining it from every angle until she got an idea about how the piece would look when it was finally restored. Then lovingly, carefully, she began to painstakingly strip off layer after layer of paint. When she reached bare wood she found that the gobs of paint had protected it so well that it didn't require much sanding at all. And when she was finished she gave this piece that she loved so much, that she made new, to me as a gift for my ordination. And most Sundays I use that stand on the altar at my church.

It seems to me that this is a lot like how God makes us new. The most important ingredient is God's love. It is God's love that sees past the layers and layers of junk and filth that I've wrapped around myself: my public image I have so carefully held on to; my habits and compulsions I rationalize away; my sin and my sins; my prejudices and hate.

And slowly, over time, God works God's love on me: peeling off a little here and a little there, and all the time knowing full well what is under all that crud. God looks at me with eyes of love and sees me as I really am, as I was created to be — and then, if I am willing, God begins to chip away and strip away what doesn't belong.

Unlike my treasured bookstand, the process with us takes a little longer — perhaps an entire lifetime. God no more strips away something than we find a substitute to fill the spot. Yet the longer God works on us and with us, the better we are able to see what God sees, and love what God loves, and begin to cooperate with the master refinisher to make all things new.

Easter 6
John 14:23-29
by Frank Ramirez

The Great Starvation Experiment

(Jesus said), "Peace I give, not as the world gives..."
— John 14:23-29

About midway between VE Day (May 8) and VJ Day (August 14) in the summer of 1945, *Life* magazine published an issue that included photographs of a starlet, the full text of the Surrender document signed by the Germans, and an editorial that warned that Russia was becoming the number one problem for Americans. Oh, and there were photographs of young Americans that might have been taken at a concentration camp. Though they were smiling at the camera they were gaunt, with their ribs sticking out, all bone and flesh with no fat.

The four-page photo spread in the July 30, 1945 issue, had the heading "Men Starve in Minnesota." It showed 36 volunteers who had voluntarily signed up to be starved nearly to death in order to teach scientists the effects of hunger and strategies for restoring starving people. These individuals were conscientious objectors who had been filtered through a rigorous screening program before being accepted. They were mostly Mennonites, Quakers, and Brethren who, because of their understanding of the words of Jesus in the Sermon on the Mount and their church's stance against war, could not take another person's life. However, all were already serving their nation in alternative service. They were anxious to demonstrate that they were as willing to take risks as those in the front line. Also, they were idealistic and looking for a way to help humanity through their service to the nation.

The rules were strict. The men were given jobs to perform and were expected to be very active, even as they received fewer and fewer calories every day. In addition to their time on the treadmill they were required to walk 22 miles outdoors, every week, regardless of the weather. Minnesota winters could be cruel.

Participants discovered that they no longer cared about literature, sports, music, and most especially women. These healthy young men lost interest in everything but food. They eagerly consumed every scrap that was given them, licking their plates clean. Their body weight dropped dramatically until they were literally skin and bones.

The program was not designed by a mad scientist, but a respected researcher who wanted to learn more about the physiology of starvation to better help those who would be rehabilitating the population of Europe when the war ended. Dr. Ancel Keys had established his reputation in medicine and nutrition with his invention of the K Ration, which provided a healthy balanced diet to soldiers in the field. Following the war, he was the researcher who established the link between diet, cholesterol, and heart disease. The massive two-volume study that resulted from the Starvation Experiment, *The Biology of Human Starvation*, is the only sanctioned study of its kind. It would no longer be ethical to produce such a study, and it has proven priceless not only for the rehabilitation of starving people, but also has provided data essential to the study of eating disorders such as anorexia.

Meanwhile, the participants were gradually restored to full health. They went on to live normal lives after the war and recovered from the experiment without any long-term health problems. They continued to serve in their churches, satisfied they had shown that the way of peace is also the way of service in the name of Jesus.

Jesus taught his apostles the way of peace, but as he said in the gospel of John, "Peace I give, not as the world gives...." The conscientious objectors believed that following the way of peace in the name of Jesus meant to be even more actively engaged in the world than before.

Ascension of Our Lord
Ephesians 1:15-23
by David O. Bales

The Eyes of the Heart Enlightened

"Why did you sleep?" the man of the family asked the boy. "All the villagers' cattle could stray — and our cow among them." He glared at the boy, who didn't answer. "These babies need milk. We took you in and gave you milk as a child. You pay us back by endangering all cows of the village."

When the boy was caught that first time he was sentenced to weeding the garden with the girls for a week — a terrible dishonor. He would never again lie down to sleep while herding the cattle. But he found a position to sit where he could sleep and appear to be alert. By sitting on something higher than the bare ground and drooping his head to his chest, from a distance his napping passed undetected. If he were to sleep any other way, an adult from the village or another shepherd would discover him and tell his family.

The boy stood now and stretched after a few heartbeats of very warm sleep. He counted the cattle through the distortion of the desert air. Nine, ten, eleven... one wandered toward the brush. The boy set out in a steady jog to circle it and haze it back. Eleven cows, one for each family. Here on the edge of the Ethiopian desert, few villages were larger. The boy knew two other villages: one was three days east into the desert, the other two days west into the striped hills.

As he ran to chase back the cow he thought about the banter in the village. Everyone was talking about them. They would come from the sky and then walk to the village. If only children spoke of such, he could disregard the news — but even the adults he lived with agreed. For twelve days the village spoke of their coming more than it complained of the extreme heat. They're coming tomorrow.

The boy shooed and switched the cattle farther for their afternoon grazing. Fortunately, here he could sit in the partial shade of a bush. He liked to get a little shade every day, especially now in the oppressive heat; but the cows always moved farther than he wanted them. If he stood right beside them, they still insisted on one step farther.

They never stayed where he led. He, however... he must follow his precise orders every day. No step further of freedom for him. Someone told him the direction and distance. The cattle had more choice than he did and when he brought the cattle home at night, people were glad only to see their cow.

He'd herded cows since his sixth summer. During his eleventh summer he was doing the same thing and living in the same borrowed home. Nothing changed. Certainly nothing got better. One thing was different today — because the desert had received one of its rare rainfalls, the boy found a puddle a handwidth across that the cows hadn't spied. He looked into its muddy water and saw the outline of his head and shoulders. Three, perhaps four years ago he'd seen his outline in a puddle. He didn't remember his head seeming as large. He could ask the woman in the family if he'd grown much in three years, but she'd probably do as usual when he talked: sigh, turn away, and begin to scrape out a pot or make bread.

The next day the boy again took the cattle where he was told. Again he sat and pretended to watch them. He closed his eyes. They'll arrive today. They've left their giant village and entered a room that flies. They're coming to teach about Jesus. The boy gladly anticipated their arrival. When the village gathered to dance and sing he felt less alone.

By the time the boy drove the cattle to the village that evening, groups of people were gathered on the field next to the village. He left each cow at its hut, then strode quickly toward a loud group of children crowded around two light-skinned men. One man stepped forward to a girl and the interpreter pointed to the light-skinned man, "Look at him. Look." Soon they bent down together to look at something the boy couldn't see and the children around screamed, "You. You. That's you." The girl laughed, trying to stop her giggling with both hands, scuffing her feet and stirring up puffs of dust. The next child said, "Me! Me!"

The boy didn't know what caused the uproar in the center of the crowd. He stood on tiptoes at the edge of the group. The lighter-skinned men wore hats with bills in front and shirts with long sleeves clinging with sweat. One light-skinned man looked over the other children to him and said something. The boy didn't understand. The light-faced man gestured with a cupped hand. The interpreter said to the boy, "Come. Come." The other children moved to let him by. A light-faced man raised the small, shiny box near his face and seemed to aim at the boy. The boy heard a click. The man turned the box around and held it down to the boy. "Look," the interpreter said. "Look here."

The boy looked at a tiny picture of a boy's face. He didn't know why the man was holding it to him or who the boy was in this vividly clear picture. He cocked his head to the side like a confused dog. The girl beside him laughed and screamed with delight, "That's you, Lema. That's you, Lema."

Lema looked at the girl beside him who was saying his name. Then Lema looked at the interpreter holding the shiny picture box. The man said, "Lema?" He pointed to the picture. "Lema, that's you. God made you, Lema, and Jesus knows your name and what you look like. And Jesus loves *you*, Lema, as though you were the only person in the world to love."

Easter 7
John 17:20-26
by Stan Purdum

In All His Glory

Father, I desire that those also, whom you have given me, may be with me where I am, to see my glory, which you have given me because you loved me before the foundation of the world.
— John 17:24

When Brittany and her seven-year-old son Brandon arrived at the play area in the park on Thursday, Jenny was already there. Thursdays were her day to watch her grandson Mark, who was also seven. As soon as the two boys were turned loose on the playground, they applied themselves vigorously to the monkey bars and swings. Jenny was already seated on a nearby park bench, and Brittany sank down wearily beside her. Despite their age difference, the two women had become friends since meeting in the park.

"Hi Brittany," Jenny said. "You look worn out."

"Oh, I am. It's getting to be such a battle with Brandon every time we go anywhere to get him to dress properly for the weather. I mean, it can't be more than 55 degrees today, but he refuses to wear a hat. He says nobody wears them at school. So there he is, hatless. You must think I'm a bad mother."

Jenny chuckled. "Not at all. Haven't you heard that old saying that 'A sweater is an item a child has to put on when his mother feels cold'?"

"That's cute, but..."

"Listen, Brittany, there must be a difference in metabolism between children and their parents. I don't know if any scientific evidence exists to verify it, but kids seem to run hotter than grown-ups. You should have seen me when

Mark's father was born. He was our first child, and I was determined to be a good mother. The first time I took him outside, I dressed him in a sleeper, a sweater, a coat, and a hat with ear flaps, and then I wrapped him in a quilted blanket."

"What's wrong with that?" Brittany asked.

"It was *July*."

Both women laughed.

"I guess I do need to lighten up a bit," Brittany said.

"Oh, you'll learn soon enough. Kids have a way of teaching us. Brandon's resisting the hat now, but wait a bit. Pretty soon he won't want to wear any of the clothes you've so lovingly selected for him. At school, what the other kids are wearing has a huge influence."

"Actually, that's already started."

"Have you gotten to the 'at least' stage yet?" Jenny asked.

"What's that?"

"It's what parents say after they realize that the dressing-the-kid battle is lost. As in 'Well, if you don't want to wear your raincoat, at least take an umbrella,' or 'If you won't wear that warm hat I bought for you, at least put on a scarf.' And then there's 'All right, you don't have to wear your mittens, but at least take them with you in your book bag.'"

"That's what's ahead? Good grief."

"The people who live next door to me have a twelve-year-old. He wears short pants every month of the year. I know his mother makes him 'at least' put on a warm jacket in cold months. I know this because he regularly leaves it behind at my house when he goes home without it after playing with Brian — that's Mark's older brother. He often comes to our house after school."

Brittany laughed despite her frustration.

Jenny continued, "The other losing battle is getting kids to dress appropriately for whatever occasion is at hand —

such as going to church. Brian and Mark's mom told me about a dust-up they had last Sunday morning when they were getting ready to go to church. She had Mark attired in dress pants and a nice sweater. But then Brian came out of his room in jeans and a T-shirt. Naturally, she told him to change, and naturally he resisted. She stood her ground, but when Brian returned, he had put on clothes only marginally better. And by that time they were running late, so they went with that. But then Mark started in with, 'If Brian gets to wear jeans, why can't I?' And it went downhill from there."

"It sounds daunting," Brittany observed.

"Well, it is, I suppose. But after a while you learn to pick your battles. Sometimes the clothes thing just isn't that important. But you do have one line of defense, you know."

"I do? Tell me."

"Kids don't do their own laundry. You do. And when they get attached to certain garments you really don't like, you have the ability to make them 'magically' disappear in the wash."

"I'll remember that," Brittany said. "Now, if we could only figure a way to make hats and mittens 'magically' appear on their heads and hands."

***

In John 17:24, Jesus prays that his followers may see his glory. Sometimes we miss his glory because we try to dress him in garments of our choosing. We dress him as the sweet, permissive savior or the enlightened sage or the "man's man" or the gentle shepherd or the super social worker or as some other favorite image. But we need to stand back and view the full image of Jesus from the scriptures. When we do, his glory will be apparent.

Pentecost Sunday
Acts 2:1-21
by C. David McKirachan

I'd Like to Thank...

I'm receiving an award tonight. That may seem like small change to most of you but other than my degrees, a bronze medal in the Mid-Atlantic Conference, and some thank you's, I've never received an award. I didn't really notice that bit of trivia until I realized I had to write an acceptance speech. I've written books, sermons, lectures, essays, poems, eulogies, research papers, treatises, and songs, but I've never written an acceptance speech. That's when it occurred to me, I'd never been given an award.

"I'd like to thank the judges and my wife and my mom..." Somehow the models that I'd gleaned from the few times I'd stumbled or been pulled into the Oscar show didn't seem to fill the bill. I was puzzled and nonplussed.

Now what the heck does all of this have to do with the second chapter of Acts? I've always thought Peter's speech after the shakin' and rattlin' has to be one of the most in-your-face, lack-of-tact, slam dunks I've ever seen or heard. Then again such slam dunks rarely win hearts or influence people. I didn't think his was a good model either.

This award is from the American Conference on Diversity. The rabbi and I are both getting it for our work in "...championing the cause of encouraging, facilitating, enhancing, and helping to create inclusive communities." There's no mention of eating, drinking, laughing, supporting, sharing family ties, or being human together. But we're getting the award anyway.

On Pentecost the diversity of the world stopped being an issue. The Spirit blew through it like tissue paper. So much for all the reservations and prejudices that had taken who knows how long to build. People didn't stop being different, it just became secondary.

Okay, maybe that was a good way to start. So I did. Here it is, you get it first.

"Three years ago, I got married. I learned that being different is good. I'm a slow learner. She's a good teacher.

"If communities of faith are to have any authenticity or integrity in this post-modern age, we must reach toward something more than a recitation of our version of history or sad litanies of dogma. We must remember that faith is an affirmation of something far beyond our understanding or our limitations. We represent the presence of something that can never be limited or boxed. These two communities of faith have had a close relationship for decades. They will never be the same. But because of their relationship and because of their difference, they learn. And because of our learning, and in the midst of it, we rejoice. And I know that our God does too. Thank you."

It's not Jack Nicholson, but it's got a flavor of Pentecost. Did you know that's a Jewish holiday too?

Holy Trinity Sunday
John 16:12-15
by Peter Andrew Smith

Guided on the Path

His grandmother was waiting for him as soon as the ordination service finished.

"John, you've come so far," she said with tears in her eyes. "I am so proud of you."

"Thanks, Gran." John shook his head. "I can't believe it's real."

"Oh, it is." She straightened his preaching stole. "I always knew that you were going to be a pastor."

"You did?"

"Certainly, I knew since you were a little boy and came to live with us."

"I wish you had said something to me," John said. "It might have made my journey here easier."

"But I did tell you on numerous occasions," she replied.

John tilted his head to one side. "I don't ever remember you saying to me that I would be a pastor."

"After the accident when you came to live with us, the first thing I told you was that God was going to help us get through the terrible loss of your parents."

"I remember that. I didn't know what it meant because I'd never really been to church before I came to live with you and Gramps." John smiled. "It's hard to believe that there was a time when I'd never been to church."

"Especially now," his grandmother said. "When you started preaching this morning it was like you had always been a preacher. That's what I saw that first year when you helped your sister come to grips with what happened."

"I didn't think I helped that much."

"Oh, you did. You were caring and supportive and you loved her as much as you could." His grandmother tapped his chest. "That's when I knew God wanted you as a pastor."

"If you knew why didn't you tell me?"

"When you were a little boy who didn't know anything about being in church?" his grandmother asked. "You wouldn't have understood what I meant."

"So you didn't actually tell me."

"No, I did. I took you to church so you could come to know God and see what a pastor did," she said. "Remember Pastor Stevens?"

"I sure do," John said. "I still remember his voice filling the church. He sure could preach."

"That he could. He was the one who encouraged you to get involved in the youth group, wasn't he?"

"Yes, he did. It was a hard year keeping that group together after he left and before Pastor LeDrew came."

"You wanted to quit more than once. Remember what I told you?"

"That good things take work and God's things take persistence," John replied. "I remembered those words through high school chemistry and when I went to join the church."

"We were so proud when you stood up front and gave your life to Christ."

"I was never so scared," John said, "to see all of those people looking at me and not wanting to disappoint them or you."

His grandmother laughed. "I thought you were going to fling the pages of the Bible loose you were shaking so badly."

"I had never spoken in front of a group before. I was terrified."

"And you got through it okay." His grandmother patted his hand. "The next time you read you weren't quite as nervous."

"I don't remember the second time I read in church."

"Christmas Eve when you couldn't find the reading from Luke and kept flipping through the Bible," she said. "You claimed after that you would never read in church again."

"I did?"

"Uh-huh. That was until Pastor LeDrew took you aside and told you the story about the time he announced a responsive psalm and then read a different one his first Sunday in a new church."

"I remember him telling me that." John laughed. "But I read in church a lot before I went to college."

"You certainly did because I wouldn't let you give up sharing that clear strong voice you have."

John narrowed his eyes. "That's how you told me I was going to be a pastor… by encouraging me to be a leader in the church."

"Telling a boy who was terrified to read in front of people that he was going to be a pastor would have been overwhelming. I pointed you in the direction I knew God was calling you and let you find the way," she said.

"The Holy Spirit was working through you."

"Me?" his grandmother said. "There was nothing holy or special about what I did. I just kept encouraging you. You're the one God is working through. You're the pastor."

"You really believe that God is working through me?" John asked.

"Of course I do and so does the church," she pointed at his robes. "You've been ordained."

"Then why don't you believe me?"

"Believe you?"

"Yes. Why don't you believe me when I say that the Holy Spirit was working in your life when you raised me?"

"But I didn't do anything special," his grandmother said.

"You took me in and helped me to know God. You guided me past my fears so I could answer my calling," John said. "I think that is special."

His grandmother waved her hand. "Lots of folks raise their children and grandchildren right."

"Does that make it any less special? I remember 'There are lots of people who follow Jesus but all of them are important in God's kingdom' being taught to me when I was a boy," John winked.

"John, you know it's not fair to use my own words to argue with me."

"They were good words for me to hear," John said. "Why aren't they good for you to hear?"

His grandmother paused. "Do you really think God used me to help make you a pastor?"

"Yes," John said. "I know it. The same as you knew I would grow up to be a pastor in the church."

His grandmother stood there and stared at him for a moment. John wrapped his arms around her. "God bless you for your faithfulness, Gran. God bless you."

Proper 4
Pentecost 2
Ordinary Time 9
1 Kings 18:20-21 (22-29) 30-39
by Keith Hewitt

Give Me an S...

The room smelled of pizza and desperation, with a hint of despair. A slice of cold pizza lay face down on the carpet, a casualty of an interception and touchdown — the same play that had caused the pizza pan to go sailing across the room, taking a nick out of the wall next to the TV and leaving behind a smudge of sauce. Marilyn scooted forward in her seat and perched at the edge while the figures on the screen lined up for a kickoff, her elbows resting on her knees, her face cradled in her hands. Her lips moved silently as she tried not to listen to the announcers' inanities.

"You have got to be kidding me!"

She jumped in her seat, head snapping up from her hands, immediately grateful that she had been to the bathroom during the official timeout. "What!?" she exclaimed, turning toward the voice. "Who the — How the —?"

The figure sitting on the couch gestured toward the TV without looking at her, said matter-of-factly, "They're down by twelve, with a minute and ten seconds left — pretty much the only way they can win is to run the kickoff back for a touchdown, recover an onside kick, and then drive down for another touchdown — all without any timeouts. Why not just part the Red Sea, while we're at it?" Eyes turned toward her, then, and the intruder's head shook slowly. "And you — seriously?"

"Seriously what? What did I do?" she demanded, forgetting the TV for a moment.

" 'O God, if you're really out there, give me a sign — let them pull this off,' " the figure — was it a man or a woman? — quoted, eyes turning upward piously at the end, before rotating back down to stare reprovingly at Marilyn. "Skipping past the 'if you're really out there' part, do you really think that's an appropriate use of prayer?"

"It's a playoff game!" Marilyn answered indignantly.

"Right. Playoff. There's an earthquake about to happen in China, North Korea is getting ready to light off another atomic bomb, and there's an airliner flying between Rio and Madrid with only one engine working — but this is a playoff. Of course you would want God's attention focused here."

"I thought God was — you know, everywhere. And all-powerful."

"Doesn't mean he can't be annoyed by all this piddlin' stuff. And for the most part he doesn't do things himself — he's kind of a big picture guy. He sends us to do them."

"So you're an —" she trailed off, hesitated.

"Yeah, that's me. An angel. And I can tell you, we don't like wasting our time." The visitor gestured toward the TV again, chided wearily, "Look, be reasonable. We don't get involved in this stuff anymore. You've gotta know people are praying for both teams. We don't pick sides — it's just not that important. It doesn't really affect your life — it shouldn't, anyway. If it does, you've got other problems."

"But I — wait, you said don't get involved in this stuff anymore?"

"That's right. If we did, Aaron Rodgers would have been MVP in 2010. But we had to let that slide."

"But you have gotten involved in it, in the past?"

The angel seemed to hesitate, then shrugged. "Well — let's just say there were some new procedures put in place after the 1967 NFL Championship. You know: Twenty below, Bart Starr, thirteen seconds left, on a quarterback sneak." The angel sighed. "Turns out, Dallas was supposed to win that game. The Old Man wasn't happy, so we had to make sure it wouldn't happen again."

There was a long pause, and then the angel went on. "And that brings me to the other reason for my visit. You said, 'O God, if you're really out there, give us a sign.' That's kind of insulting."

"How is that insulting? I'm expressing a rational question, a rational doubt —"

A raspberry from the visitor cut her off. "A sign? You want a sign?" the angel continued. "How about looking up at the sky or looking really closely at a flower? Entropy says things go from a more ordered state to a less ordered state — but, somehow, the universe went from chaos to a much higher ordered state. So take a deep breath or listen to your own heartbeat — you are an impossible marvel."

Marilyn frowned, looked puzzled, but didn't say anything.

"Look, you people, you're always asking for a sign — it's a constant game of what-have-you-done-for-me-lately. 'God, listen to me — if you don't do what I want you to, I won't believe in you.' You wonder why God has gray hair in all your paintings of him? It's because of you!" The angel waved a hand toward the outside world. "The rest of the universe is all neat and orderly — a wonder. But you people have to question it. You have to question him. It's like you're reading a book, but because you can't actually see the author standing in front of you, you're not really sure anybody wrote it."

Marilyn looked down. "I'm sorry. I didn't mean it that way."

"Maybe, maybe not, but that's how it came out. It's hurtful."

"I'm sorry," she repeated. "It's just — you know, this is important to me."

"God really does answer prayers, Marilyn, but the purpose isn't to prove himself to you. The purpose is to grant those who believe in him some small graces, from time to time — and also to show his power and glory to those who don't believe. You know, Daniel in the lion's den, Elijah versus the priests of Baal, that sort of thing."

She blinked. "What?"

"Never mind. You know, it wouldn't hurt you to sign up for a Bible study — I'm just saying. It would look good on the ol' permanent record."

Marilyn's eyebrows drew together. "What do you mean?"

"Never mind. The point is, God isn't Cris Angel or Lance Burton, performing wonders for your amusement. There has to be meaning, otherwise it's pointless. But I wanted to come by and let you know you were heard."

"Oh — well... thank you. I guess."

The angel nodded. "No problem. And now, if you'll excuse me, I have a few thousand more stops to make." As the figure of the angel faded, the head shook slowly. "I hate the playoffs," the angel muttered, the voice hanging in the air afterward.

Marilyn hesitated, straining to see as the image went away, finally shook her head and turned to the TV once more. Somehow, it didn't seem quite as important, now.

But she did wait for the clock to run out before she turned it off...

Just in case.

Proper 5
Pentecost 3
Ordinary Time 10
1 Kings 17:8-16
by Rick McCracken-Bennett

Oh God...
Please Don't Make Me Go!

John was reluctantly beginning to sense that his time at First Church was drawing to a close. Reluctantly, because he loved the church, he loved the people, he loved the work they did in the community in Christ's name — and because, he had to admit, he could do his work in his sleep.

And that was probably it... that he realized that he hadn't done anything new there, preached any new word, or led the church into a new vision of God's call to them in a very long time. He had told others facing the same situation that churches need different gifts at different parts of their life cycle. He really believed that but only when it applied to others. Certainly he had the gifts necessary for the next phase of life at First Church. Or if he didn't, he could learn them.

Still, it was bothering him enough that he took Bill, a lay leader in the congregation, to breakfast to tell him what was on his mind. "So you're thinking you might be called to go somewhere else — probably some bigger, better place in your mind," said Bill. "You know, I would believe in this 'calling' business a little more if just one of you took a 'call' that paid you less than the place you were leaving!"

Maybe it was Bill's criticism or maybe it was really the call of God — but John took a call to a little, dying church in a little, dying community. The pay cut was one thing, the loss of other benefits still another, but the biggest loss of all was the loss of prestige.

Being the pastor of First Church came with many perks — Rotary Club membership, a golf membership at the country club, a seat on the United Way board. Now the most he received was a clergy discount at the mom and pop restaurant in town. It was also quite a blow to go from preaching to 850 people to preaching to 45 or 50 on a good Sunday.

The village of his new little church was soul-sick and very tired. The closing of the wheel-bearing plant drove many out of town, and the drought that had lasted for several years now threatened to bankrupt just about everybody else.

Every night John would pray that God would reveal to him why he was sent to this God-forsaken place. Was he only here to officiate over the burial of the church and maybe even the town? Was he being tested? And even though he knew better, he asked God what he had done to offend God and deserve this.

The only thing he thought he heard back was "love them." That was it, just "love them."

The folks there were generous and asked him over to dinner just about every night of the week. Certainly they didn't have enough money to put on such a meal but each and every one was a meal fit for a king. And the collection — it was not what you would expect. Nothing like First Church, mind you, but generous. You might call it the "widow's mite." And John did love them and pleaded to God for them and asked them to sacrifice for those less fortunate.

Before his first year was out, the church had stocked a pantry for those in need, served breakfast each weekday for the elderly, and begun an after-school tutoring program. All John kept saying was, "We need to do the work God has given us to do. God will provide. God will take care of us." He said it even when he had a hard time believing it.

The funny thing is, John's new church didn't die. As they sacrificed so dearly so that others would not have to suffer as much, God richly blessed them.

On Rogation Day, John and thirty or so of his parishioners went around the village and their part of the county blessing the fields and praying for seasonable weather. Specifically, they were praying for rain. Farmers would get off their tractors and join in the prayers. They had to believe that their God would save them. If he didn't… well, if God didn't, the outcome would be worse than most could bear.

In June, after all the crops had been planted, the rain began; a slow, soaking, wonderful rain that lasted for several days and then returned every few days or so. People declared that it was a miracle. Perhaps it was. But the bigger miracle was that John's faith was strengthened each and every day as he remembered the great works God had done in the lives of those people.

Oh yes… the church grew, too. It never became huge in size but it became large enough for them to double their efforts to serve those in need with what they themselves had been given. The drought was truly over.

Proper 6
Pentecost 4
Ordinary Time 11
1 Kings 21:1-10 (11-14) 15-21a
by David O. Bales

The Mayor's Wife

I only contacted you because she's gone too far, to an extreme that can't be imagined; and she does it so stealthily. I need someone who'll take seriously what only a few of us know fully: the depths this woman has sunk to.

I need your oath. Swear that what I say is completely off the record. My information must be anonymous. Agreed?

Good question. I chose you because of some things you've reported in the paper and because you're new in town. No one who's lived here long keeps a neutral perspective when it comes to the mayor and Mrs. Moore. You'll have to believe me, and I'll have to trust you.

You going to take out paper and pencil?

Tape recorder? I don't know. I don't want my voice in this. I'm serious about not being identified. Yes, tape is more accurate. But give me your word that when you transcribe this you'll destroy the tape. Paranoid, you think. I can tell. Well, listen and decide.

Robert D. Moore Sr. was mayor for twenty years, and now Robert D. Jr. has reigned for another sixteen. The behavior of Robert Jr.'s wife, Diane Moore, must be exposed. I've been around since the beginning of Old Bob's reign. He started the political plums and pork. Graft: dishonest, impure graft. He got kickbacks and protection money from anyone who worked for or around the city. The chief of police was in his pocket, and most council members too. But, and this is the point, Old Bob distributed money in all directions. By being free with his favors and only keeping a fraction of his gains, he became more and more secure in office.

But Young Robert D. didn't begin that way. That family attribute had to be acquired through marriage instead of by DNA. Diane worked for Old Bob in his last two administrations, and he handpicked her for his son.

Don't you see? Old Bob as much as trained her to take over, since he wanted his son and not a daughter-in-law to be the next mayor.

You're new in town. All you know about Mrs. Moore is her charities. She follows the "small percentage" theory of her father-in-law. She takes a lot, distributes most in favors, and maintains her philanthropic façade, but even a small slice of her extortion and blackmail is a great deal. Last week your paper displayed her on the front page with another charity for disabled children. Her goal is to be pictured at least once a month in your paper. Most people know her that way.

No, never had children. Don't think they tried.

Technically, she's his secretary. But she directs the mayor. If he gives an order when she's not there, they wait and phone her to check what she wants. Few city workers don't owe her favors. Or she holds knowledge of an indiscretion over them like an anvil ready to drop if they don't tow the line.

Her photo in your paper kicked me over the edge. I was at that event. Had to be there — all shirt-and-tied up. I'd just come from the courthouse where she as much as celebrated her greatest victory. She did it her way, not with balloons and banners, but with a smirk. The mayor's door was open. I saw her smile in the mayor's office. I saw her newspaper smile and that did it.

Twelve years ago Terence Bailey was elected as district attorney. He was Young Bob's pick, and he won handily. He followed orders for the first two years. Then, even though he wasn't breaking open the organization, he started prosecuting cases he shouldn't. She warned him — politely, of course. He did it anyway. Not a huge rebellion. He argued that he must prosecute some flagrant crimes. If he didn't, the whole administration would rip apart from public outcry.

As far as Mrs. Moore was concerned that wasn't his call. I was walking out of the mayor's office when word came Bailey was making his first forbidden prosecution. Mrs. Moore said, "Oh he is, is he?" She smiled that left-handed little smile, and I knew she'd break him if it took half her fortune and the rest of her life.

Last week... What was that? Over there. Sounded like somebody. Didn't you hear something? Guess I'm jumpy.

Last week's newspaper with her picture included the story of Bailey's resignation. I've got my suspicions of how she did it. When your paper was delivered to his desk, Young Bob held it up so she'd see her picture on the front page. She said, "Give me that." She thumbed to the second page, dropped the paper onto his desk, pointed to "D.A. Resigns," smiled slightly, touched her finger to her temple, and walked into her office. She got him. Took her ten years.

Don't look so skeptical. No, I can't *prove* it. I'm telling you we're dealing here not with just an evil person but with intelligent wickedness. You can dig around a little. I think you'll find others who might say a few things — some older guys nearest to retirement, particularly in the city streets department. We took flak from the public when they caught us blacktopping the mayor's driveway.

Will you look into it? And I need your word that you'll transcribe this and not include my name. No matter if Young Bob loses the next election, Mrs. Moore is owed enough favors and knows enough secrets to rule this city until she dies. I have your word that you'll look into this?

117

*This document was discovered in a manila envelope behind a file cabinet when the **Herald** newspaper building was sold. Included was the following portion of a newspaper article:*

WIDOW OF EX-MAYOR HONORED

Mrs. Diane Moore, 94, was laid to rest Saturday in the largest funeral since….

Proper 7
Pentecost 5
Ordinary Time 12
1 Kings 19:1-18
by Scott Dalgarno

7 - 7-7-77

It might be called a "slam dunk" today. The prophet Elijah faced down Ahab, the king of Israel; his spitfire of a wife, Jezebel; and along with them, 100 prophets of Baal. There on top of Mount Carmel he made fools of them all and showed once and for all who was God in Israel.

And then, wonder of wonders, what can only be called a great depression settled upon the prophet; a "darkness visible" to use the words of the novelist William Styron. Instead of exulting, the prophet slunk off to a cave like an African pachyderm waiting for his end.

The story of such a splendid hero reaching his lofty goal and then crashing shortly after is, yes, hard to understand but it also happens to be quite common. Here is an account of one such modern hero.

On the seventh day of the seventh month in 1977, at seven in the evening, Englishman Harold Abrahams dined for the last time with his compatriot Arthur Porritt. They had met for dinner at the hour of 7 p.m. on the seventh day of July every year since that lucky date in 1924 when Porritt and Abrahams knelt, nearly shoulder to shoulder, at the beginning of what Abrahams would later call "the loneliest ten seconds of my life."

That day, in Paris, the two managed to bring more honor to England than any two athletes in the island's glorious history. Abrahams won the gold medal in the 100-meter and Porritt took home the bronze. To the joy of every European in attendance, they ran the favored American champion, Charlie Paddock, off his feet. The race was greeted with such joy in England that (along with the success of their teammate Eric Liddell in the 400 meters) they managed to raise the status of track and field on Shakespeare's sceptered isle from a minor to a major sport. Would the Oxfordian Roger Bannister have broken the four-minute mile thirty years later without them? Probably not.

So what caused "the fastest man in the world" to go into such a steep mental decline in the wake of his greatest triumph? Perhaps it was the same thing that drove him so hard to excel. Running wasn't a passion for Harold Abrahams, it was a self-confessed compulsion. Harold Abrahams ran not because he loved to run but because he hated being Jewish.

More than anything else, he wanted his ethnicity not to matter in an age and country where it mattered way too much. It was as if he always had an asterisk after his name. Even when he met the Prince of Wales after his great victory he felt that he wasn't the gold medalist from England — he was the Semite medalist. In a word, for Harold Abrahams, running was a "weapon," a weapon he could wield against all the self-satisfied English he believed were his true opponents in life. It was anger at them and what he believed they thought of him that fueled him as he tore down that 4 foot x 100 meter strip of real estate that made his name in British athletic history.

It was also that anger that made him do something no British Olympic sprinter in history had ever done — hire a personal trainer. Sprinters had run forever on heart. Harold Abrahams was the first Englishman to run with his brains. In the 1920 Olympics, Abrahams had failed in the quarterfinals of both the 100 and 200 meters. He hadn't come even close. Four years later he was a different kind of runner. His first afternoon at the oval with Sam Mussabini had changed everything. Born in London of Arab, Turkish, French, and

Italian ancestry, Mussabini, like Abrahams, was *persona non grata* with his nation's athletic elite. That made the two all the more a team. They'd show the Cambridge snobs Abrahams went to school with what a champion looked like.

Mussabini was able to spot Abraham's troubles immediately. "You're overstriding," he said. Big strides were fine for distance but they meant death for the sprinter. That bit of wisdom, along with the advice that Abrahams should focus on the 100 meter race and a sensible training regimen were just what the Jewish sprinter needed. That and one more thing: a proper attitude as he peered down the lonely 100 meters.

By the time of the big Olympic day (7 p.m. on July 7, 1924), Abrahams admitted to butterflies — gargantuan butterflies. A self-confessed neurotic, he said that for four years he'd been so afraid of the thought of losing; now (he could hardly believe it) he found himself just as terrified at the prospect of winning. Mussabini had an answer for that too: "Only think of two things — the gun and the tape. When you hear the one, just run like hell until you break the other."

And he did. Harold Abrahams won. And after the initial exultation came the plummeting. He had worked so hard. He had dreamed of the moment for so very long. He had proved so much, and still, he had come up... empty. Was it simply a case of doing the right thing for the wrong reason? No one could say but Harold Abrahams — and he wasn't talking.

In time he got over it. Marriage to a good woman helped. So did breaking his leg in competition the next year. He had nothing left to prove anyway, and now he could devote himself to the law and a new side career — sports journalism. The British public adored hearing him on BBC, and they told him so.

Most importantly, once he'd proved himself on the track and made peace with a new life off of it, he began to hear a still small voice — a voice that told him it was time to make

121

peace with his ethnicity. He had tried hating being Jewish — that hadn't worked. Why not try embracing it? He did and in time he became president of the Jewish Athletic Association.

At 7 p.m. in the evening on July 7, 1977 (7-7-77), Harold Abrahams and his friend Arthur Porritt dined together for the last time. They were old men now. They had known what it meant to fly high, and they knew what it meant to come back down to the ground. Abrahams knew what it meant to hit it hard, but he also knew how to bounce. Resilience was the key to happiness — that and not taking yourself too seriously. He would leave that to others. He was happy to die forgotten. Little did he know that in five years the world would take note of his Olympic triumph in the Academy Award-winning film *Chariots of Fire*.

Proper 8
Pentecost 6
Ordinary Time 13
Luke 9:51-62; Psalm 77:1-2, 11-20
by Argile Smith

Confidence in Crisis

Regina and Sam enjoyed watching movies together. They liked "cliffhangers" most of all, the kind that kept them sitting on the edges of their seats from the first flash of the story on the screen until the first frame of the credits. One day at work, they decided to take in one of the summer action thrillers that had just been released. The movie previews boasted a lineup of top-shelf superstars, and the take-your-breath-away storyline promised to be nail-biting, to say the least. They could hardly wait until the Saturday afternoon matinee.

On Friday afternoon, Sam overheard a conversation outside his office door. Two people at work were talking about the movie that he and Regina planned to see the next day. Although he didn't want to eavesdrop for fear that the information would ruin the fun for himself and Regina, he simply couldn't resist the temptation. He listened in and found out how the movie ended.

Not wanting to disappoint Regina, who had been looking forward to the chance to see the movie that had been getting such rave reviews, Sam kept what he had heard outside his office door to himself. On Saturday afternoon the two of them made their way to the cinema, bought their tickets, loaded up on popcorn and sodas, and sat in their favorite seats, ready to experience a movie buff's version of a roller-coaster ride.

Regina sat munching her popcorn and anticipating the thrill of what would happen next, thanks to all sorts of twists and turns in the unfolding story. Sitting next to her, Sam registered a little less anticipation. After all, he knew how the movie would end before it started.

The movie turned out to live up to the reviews. Regina hardly had time to settle into her seat before one shocking surprise after another jolted her. Like other good movies, the flick throttled her imagination into hyper-drive. At every twist or turn, her mind raced ahead of the story to figure out how it would end. By contrast, Sam sat there, enjoying the movie but not getting anxious about how the story would turn. He registered a quiet confidence that everything would work out just fine. As Regina whispered her hunches about how the story would end to Sam, he sat quietly and chuckled under his breath.

At one point in particular, there were hints that the lead character might be killed off in a chase scene involving nuclear-powered jet airplanes streaking across the sky like lightning bolts, weaving and in and out of mountain ranges with laser guns blazing. Sam didn't take the hint seriously, however, and for one good reason: he already knew that the hero wouldn't be killed. In fact, he even knew that the hero would win the day and give the movie a hand-clapping happy ending.

At the end of the movie, Sam confessed to Regina that he had kept what he overheard about the movie from her. His confession helped her to understand why he didn't get anxious as the story unfolded. His confidence had come from what he knew.

The Psalmist wrote about his quiet confidence in the Lord as he faced the twists and turns in his life. Likewise, Jesus reflected a deep sense of confidence as he faced the rejection of the Samaritans, the angry prejudices of the disciples, and the wafer-thin devotion of people who wanted to follow him. His confidence came from what he knew.

Proper 9
Pentecost 7
Ordinary Time 14
2 Kings 5:1-14
by Sandra Herrmann

Being Helped in Spite of Himself

> *Elisha sent a messenger to Naaman, saying, "Go, wash in the Jordan seven times, and your flesh shall be restored and you shall be clean." But Naaman became angry and went away, saying, "I thought that for me he would surely come out, and stand and call on the name of the Lord his God, and would wave his hand over the spot, and cure the leprosy! Are not Abana and Pharpar, the rivers of Damascus, better than all the waters of Israel? Could I not wash in them, and be clean?" He turned and went away in a rage.* — 2 Kings 5:10-12

"Jenny, call the travel agency, please. I need to leave on the first available flight to Norway. I'll need a hotel the first night but after that I'll be living on an oil rig. I won't need a car; the oil company's picking me up and delivering me."

"I'll get right on it, Mr. Daniels." Jenny called the agency and asked for her favorite agent. Sarah had taught Jenny the ins and outs of booking flights, and Jenny had taught Sarah what services her boss wanted. It was a perfect working relationship, one that Sarah had worked to establish. Unfortunately, Sarah was helping another customer at the moment.

"I can have her call you as soon as she's done," the receptionist told Jenny. No need to leave a number; Jenny and Sarah were in each other's rolodexes.

Jenny went back to working on the papers on her desk.

A few minutes later, Mr. Daniels strode out of his office, and stopped short. "What are you doing, Jenny? I need that reservation, and I need it right now!" He was red in the face and scowling. Even the papers in his hand were shaking.

"Mr. Daniels!" Jenny was shocked. Her boss had never treated her this way. Something must be wrong. But when she asked, he shook the papers in her direction and ordered her to "Make that call! Right now!"

"I already have, Mr. Daniels. Sarah, our usual agent, was helping another customer. She'll get back to me in just another minute or so."

"Why on earth would you need to have Sarah? Any agent can book a flight. Now get on it!"

Jenny looked down for a second, and then nodded. "I'm calling even as we speak."

Apparently satisfied, Mr. Daniels stomped back into his office. Jenny waited as long as she thought she could, listening for Mr. Daniels as she did so. An extra minute would possibly assure that she could get Sarah on the job.

Just as she had dialed, Mr. Daniels was back at her desk. "Well?" he demanded.

Jenny held up her index finger to show him she was waiting for the phone to be answered. When the connection was made, she asked the receptionist, "Is Sarah available yet? Oh, good. Yes, I can hold." She winked and nodded at Mr. Daniels, who was still standing at her desk.

"Hold? Jenny, this is possibly the most important trip I'm taking this year. And you're on HOLD? Why, may I ask? And it had better not be that you're holding for Sarah. Get hold of an agent and do it now!"

"Mr. Daniels," Jenny said in her best professional, calming voice, "I don't know why you're so angry. You only told me five minutes ago that you need this flight. It always takes about ten minutes to do a booking. And Sarah is the best person in that office. I trust her to do all of the travel plans that we need, and she's never let us down."

Mr. Daniels stopped pacing and shaking but he was still a bit red around the edges.

"You remember your last trip to Sweden? She was the one who found the artist your wife is so fond of and got you that wonderful print to take home."

Mr. Daniels was beginning to look sheepish. "Was she the one who did that? I thought you did that."

"Well, we both get credit for that one. I remembered the artist's name, and she knew which gallery carried his work. Trust me, Mr. Daniels. We want Sarah to book your trip and hotel. She always gets it right, even the extras."

"Well, all right," he said grudgingly, "Get her on the job as soon as possible." He was no longer stomping as he returned to his office.

Jenny was never so glad to hear anyone's voice as she was to hear Sarah's. "How can I help you today, Jenny?"

"Oh, Sarah, Mr. Daniels needs to get on the first available flight to the North Sea. Something's brewing on an oil rig up there, and he's really anxious. I've never seen him so uptight."

So Sarah made all the arrangements, including a cab to pick up his suitcase before picking him up and delivering him to the plane. "Oh, and Jenny, should I have a box of his favorite chocolates on the table in his room when he gets there?"

Jenny smiled. As she had told Mr. Daniels, Sarah always came through. Even with the "extras."

Proper 10
Pentecost 8
Ordinary Time 15
Luke 10:25-37; Psalm 82
by Rick McCracken-Bennett

Where Have All the Good Samaritans Gone?

Jesus said, "A man was going down from Jerusalem to Jericho, and fell into the hands of robbers..." — Luke 10:30

Save the weak and the orphan; defend the humble and needy; rescue the weak and the poor; deliver them from the power of the wicked. — Psalm 82:3-4

The way I figure it, sermons ought to be done by Friday morning. If I don't have it ready by noon on Friday I go into a slow but urgent panic.

This particular Friday, though, I didn't have a clue. The weekend was already packed and there wouldn't be a moment to work on it. Life got in the way of my preparation, and I knew I had some heavy lifting to do that morning or things might not go well that Sunday morning.

The office wouldn't work; the week had been filled with distractions that promised to continue. So I left home early with legal pads, lectionary helps, a jotted note or two, and I drove to my favorite coffee shop. It was never quiet but somehow I always seemed to get work done there.

As I approached I found myself behind a van going at about minus ten miles an hour. "This is just how my week's been going," I said, punctuating it with a palm hit to the steering wheel. As often happens though, this van had a reason — a good one. She was driving on about the worst flat I had ever seen; tire shredded and rolled under, the rim carving a groove in the pavement.

She made it... sort of, into the parking lot. Parked... sort of, and as I slid into a slot nearby the woman got out with her three kids in tow. It was probably the worst flat she had ever seen as well.

So... my dilemma was to help her and not get my sermon done or get my sermon done and feel (appropriately) guilty for days. Reluctantly I decided to help, and I prayed a quick prayer to God asking that I not be too embarrassed by my preaching effort on Sunday. Maybe this wouldn't take too long.

But of course, it did. As I found the jack and the spare that hadn't been off the van in ten or so years and blocked the wheels with bricks I had in my car (don't ask!), I began to get the story.

Careful to spare her daughters a description of the brutal truth they had all experienced, she told me a little of her story. She was recently divorced, and I got the idea that it was a nasty one. She had her daughters and little else. They were on their way across the state to her sister's, where they hoped they could get a new start and enough distance from the mess they were leaving behind to have some bit of hope in a better life. And then came the flat — the proverbial straw.

I began to resent the hundred or so cars that streamed through the drive-through line without so much as a query as to whether we needed help. I might have done the same thing before that morning, but not now; never again I promised myself.

Eventually I finished, put the ripped-up tire in its place, gave her directions, refused her offer of money, and went inside, where I washed my hands, wiped some of the tire crud off my shirt, ordered a coffee, and just sat there, not knowing what in the world I would preach about.

She and her daughters came out of the restroom and walked over to my table. "Girls," she said, "I want you to remember something about what happened here this morning. Do you remember the story of the good Samaritan? Remember? We read it just a few weeks ago." They all nodded. "Well, this man is our good Samaritan. While others went on by, ignoring our situation, he helped us."

I told her that the amazing thing was that the gospel for that coming Sunday was the story about the good Samaritan, and that I had come there to write my sermon. I thought for a moment and asked if I could tell this story. She said, of course. And the girls all thanked me. The little one gave me a hug, and I held back tears until they left and drove away.

I wasn't a real "good Samaritan," not even close. My feelings about this interruption to my day reminded me that I wasn't as "good" a person as I tried to appear. But that day, that morning, whatever I was — or became as God and this woman and her kids and I converged — felt good. And miracle of miracles, I had my sermon.

And I wonder… who was really the good Samaritan that morning and who was neighbor to whom? I think I know. And I know it wasn't me.

Proper 11
Pentecost 9
Ordinary Time 16
Luke 10:38-42
by David O. Bales

Housewarming Warning

"We need four of the medium-sized canopies. I don't know the exact dimensions, but I've seen them at other parties. Look at where I want them and you figure out the size. One here." Betty Jo pointed to the front yard and continued to walk to the side of the house. "One here." She rounded the corner to the backyard. "And two here: one on each side of the patio."

"I think I can handle that," Steve said. He started across the lawn to his pickup, parked in the driveway.

"And Steve," Betty Jo said as she followed him, "I phoned them a month ago and they said they had dozens, so make sure to reserve them in white. I've seen multicolored canopies and they look like a circus."

"Right," Steve said. He groaned as he stepped into his pickup. Through the open window he yelled across the lawn, "I thought we retired and moved away to cut down our workload!"

Betty Jo laughed and shooed him away.

Betty Jo sat at the kitchen table and sorted through photos from the florist. Which arrangement would look best in the living room? In the dining room? Low centerpieces for the tables outside under the canopies. The phone rang.

"Hi Karen," Betty Jo said. "How's my faithful ex-neighbor? Tickets arrived. Great, and I've got your reservations at the Shiloh Inn. Check in Friday and out on Monday. I got a note from the Lairds. They're coming too. Like old home week.

"Yeah. I thought about it, but I'll be exhausted after Saturday. And really, we haven't looked too much this last month, living in a motel and all. But at least by being here for six weeks we got to see the last three and a half weeks of construction. You'll love it. Lawn and landscaping came almost instantly this week. The fellow who rolled down the turf said it isn't a wonderful idea to have a housewarming party on it so soon but with careful watering all summer it'll take root no matter what.

"Sure. Get settled and the party over, we'll find a church and a Bible study or a prayer group. We don't have the time yet.

"You sound like Steve. I just haven't had time. If you want to worship here Sunday, look in the telephone book and find the church. Tell the group to keep praying for me.

"Okay, looking forward to seeing you too and getting all our, dare I say, *old* neighbors from the land of the Umpqua together with our new neighbors."

Betty Jo was teetering on a stool, putting up crepe paper when Steve arrived. "We've got five days till the party," he said. "Do we need streamers up all week?"

Betty Joe put the tape in his hand, pointed him to the ceiling, and went back to the stove. "Ice. I just remembered," she said. "How about if you ask Lorna and… and… I forgot her husband's name."

"Phil."

"Yes, Phil. Why don't you walk over to Lorna and Phil's and ask them to get 27 sacks of ice for us on Saturday morning. That'll give us three sacks at the end of each canopy."

"24."

"What?"

"Twenty-four sacks. Four canopies, times two ends, times three sacks is 24."

"Oh, you tell them what to do." She smiled and waved him out the door.

She stirred furiously, one pan after another, all four burners producing meatballs, freezer containers on the counter waiting to store them until Saturday. The phone rang. "This is like the neighborhood's prayer group arriving by telephone. Karen Gillis just phoned. They're coming. How about you guys? Wonderful! I'll make reservations along with Karen and Ed. Please, I want to.

"Karen asked me too. Not yet. We get this party over and, sure enough, we'll have time to find a church. Can't live without that. You and Kent can worship Sunday morning with Karen and Ed. Scope it out for us. Let us know what you think so we can drop in there on a Sunday real soon."

The front door shut. "Steve's here. Got to put him back to work. Talk with you later."

She dashed from the phone to the stove and quickly stirred one pot after the other. With the back of her wrist she pushed hair up her forehead. She turned to Steve and said, "I'm a little diz…"

* * *

Betty Jo felt as though she had wakened and gone back to sleep a dozen times. She looked to the ceiling and didn't see streamers up yet. No streamers. Wrong walls. White. Steve was sitting in a chair next to her, holding her hand. He was slumped and unshaven. She tried to talk but felt a mask over her mouth and nose. She managed to open her eyes wider. Steve was laughing. No, he was crying.

When she woke again Betty Jo's mind was clearer, although she felt she was struggling up from the bottom of a swimming pool to become fully awake. Steve was asleep in the chair to the left of her bed. She heard a "beep beep" and looked up to a television monitor with her vital signs making lines across it. She slept again.

On the evening that Steve said was her third in intensive care she was fully lucid. Steve pulled aside the oxygen mask. She whispered to him that the party was off. He laughed as he stroked her hair. She smiled through two streaks of tears.

The next night, Steve stepped toward the bed. "Karen's on the phone and she's calling from the prayer group."

Betty Jo fumbled until she got the oxygen mask up. She motioned to Steve that she didn't want to talk. She smiled weakly and said, "Tell them, 'Okay, I have the time now.' "

Proper 12
Pentecost 10
Ordinary Time 17
Hosea 1:2-10
by Craig Kelly

I Have Loved You...

He instinctively flinched as the spit stung his eye.

"I HATE YOU! I HATE YOU! I WANT YOU DEAD! DEAD, YOU HEAR ME? YOU CAN'T DO THIS TO ME!"

As he rubbed his spit-coated eye, he was suddenly knocked into the bare white wall, leaving him momentarily dazed. When the haze cleared, he snapped his head up, fully expecting to see a fist rushing toward his face. What he saw, however, jarred him just as much as that fist would have.

The force that had knocked him over was actually two men dressed completely in white rushing into the room to wrestle the spitter down onto the hospital bed, wrapping leather restraints around her wrists and ankles as she flailed about frantically, desperately trying to escape, perhaps to try to make good on her threat.

The sight of his wife tied down to a hospital bed stung worse than the spit. He turned away, his tears washing his eyes clean. He had known for a while that this had to be done, but knowing didn't make it any easier. He found himself leaning back against that white wall, using it to brace himself, fighting the urge to collapse into a heap of tears and despair on the cold, linoleum floor.

Behind him, he could still hear the cacophony of screams and expletives, with the clang of the restraints against the metal bed railing providing a chaotic rhythm. With the euphoria of her high now fully dispelled, the true music of her heart was now being played at full volume. No love, no joy, no peace, just chaos. Such was the woman he loved.

This drug rehab facility had promised "tough love," doing whatever it takes to break the spell that drugs had placed on their patients. However, seeing his wife in restraints screaming in agony, he didn't know if this tough love was aimed at the patient or the patient's loved ones. He looked back at her in her bed, knowing that if he could somehow take her place and free her from all of this, he would.

The screams eventually died down, replaced instead by quiet sobbing. She looked up at him, her eyes, now streaming with tears, filled with a pleading desperation instead of the red-hot rage that had been there not long before.

"Baby, please, please, let's just go home. I promise I'll be good. Things will be back to the way they were before. I'll be good to you, baby. I'll be so good. Just let me go home. I won't touch the stuff again, I swear." Her head fell back against the pillow, her tears soaking into the stark white pillow cover.

Just the way they were before? His mind went back through the years of their marriage. He knew she had a history when he married her. Yet all he could see was the goodness in her, the beauty. He loved her with an intense, white-hot, no-holds-barred love. It didn't make sense, but it wasn't supposed to. He chose her, not because of what she had done or even who she was, but just because he loved her. Did he need another reason?

And yet, practically from day one, her heart was not there with him. She *needed* — she *craved* — the drugs, the other men, the life away from him. He offered order; she wanted chaos. Even the child "they" had symbolized this faithlessness. He had no Asian in his ancestry, and yet his "son" had almond-shaped eyes. And still, he took that child in as his own. He knew the child wasn't his, yet he loved him with all the love he would give to his own son.

She would disappear for weeks, months at a time, hanging out with pimps and drug lords, catering to their every whim, desperate for another hit. He would drive through every dark alleyway and side street looking for her. At times, he would even see her leaning on a car, dressed in a tight, revealing top, short mini-skirt, fishnet stockings, and stiletto heels, selling herself to some nameless john. After a while, she would come home bruised, beaten, and half-naked, hoping he would take her in. And through the hurt and the rage — yes, *rage* — he felt, he still had that burning love for her. He would yell at her, scream, cajole, and even plead with her. Every time, after a while, he would find her gone, doing the same thing all over again. Every night he would cry himself to sleep, his arm reaching across the bed, longing to feel her body there, shuffling over to cuddle with him.

She wanted things to go back to the way they used to be? His blood began to boil. The white in the room began to turn deep crimson. *She wants to use me again? She wants to just keep me on a string, carrying me along while she does whatever she pleases? Does she not know the depths of my feelings, the passion of my love for her? Does she not know what I have continued to bring her out of, how I would keep taking her in time and time again? How can she keep doing this to me? NO! NOT THIS TIME!*

A guttural scream escaped his lips as he raised his hand to strike her. Her eyes grew wide and she began to tremble as she anticipated the pain of the blow across her face. His hand stayed up for what seemed like an eternity as she could see the rage that was once in her eyes now transferred to his.

His tears continued to stream down his deep red cheeks, practically ready to boil under the heat of his rage. Yet his hand started to lower. She started to smile, thinking his anger might pass once again.

Then he struck her.

When she was with the pimps and dealers, she had often been beaten. She had suffered broken limbs, rapes, deep lacerations, the works. More than once, she had been left for dead.

Yet this slap in the face hurt. It really *hurt*.

Without saying a word, he turned his back and walked out of the room. She looked up as she saw him walk out of the room and turn a corner. She wanted to scream after him, telling him to go to hell, but the words stuck in her throat. All she could do was lay her head back on her pillow and wail.

* * *

He looked somberly down at his desk. The legal papers were still there, sitting silently in front of him, waiting patiently. They had all the time in the world. At the top, printed in ink as black as midnight:

PETITION FOR DISSOLUTION OF MARRIAGE

His mind drifted back to the words he had heard hours (*Was it really hours?*) earlier: "As your attorney and as your friend, you've got to end this. Cut her off. Spare yourself this agony."

He looked up at the framed picture sitting on his desk. His wife was smiling broadly, the smile reaching, it seemed, from ear to ear. She was in her wedding dress, the white train flowing for what seemed like miles. Her hair was in a very becoming up-do, the brilliance of the red showing even through the veil. Her eyes sparkled like perfectly cut diamonds. She was radiant.

End it? Cut her off? Could he do it? Should he? He thought back to her wedding dress, the gleam in her eyes, her smile as she walked down the aisle. He remembered the love that pulsed through him like electricity that day. He thought back to the way his heart jumped every time he looked at her.

Slowly, he rose from his desk and walked over to one of the bookshelves that lined the walls of his study. He turned on the small bookshelf stereo and pressed the PLAY button on the CD player. The room was soon filled with the flowing strings and perfect choral harmonies of Bach's *Mass in B Minor*. He collapsed back in his chair, tilted his head back, and let the music flow through him.

He loved her. Even now, he loved her. All he wanted was to have her in his arms again, to wipe the past clean and start all over. He wanted to know that she would have the same heart for him that he had for her. He just wanted to love her.

But she hurt him. She cut him. She bruised him. He loved her, and she spurned him again, and again, and again. How much more of this could he really take? He knew that right now she couldn't be faithful if she tried.

But he loved her.

After a short while, the choir began to sing the *Agnus Dei*:

Agnus Dei, qui tollis peccata mundi,
miserere nobis.
Agnus Dei, qui tollis peccata mundi,
miserere nobis.
Agnus Dei, qui tollis peccata mundi,
dona nobis pacem.

Lamb of God, who takes away the sins of the world, have mercy upon us.
Lamb of God, who takes away the sins of the world, have mercy upon us.
Lamb of God, who takes away the sins of the world, grant us peace.

Have mercy upon us. Give us your peace. Take us back. Take me back. Forgive me.

His tears fell on the divorce papers, making the ink start to run. All he could do was sit there and cry.

Take me back. Forgive me.

Slowly he rose, wiping his face. Taking the tear-stained papers, he walked over to the corner of the room. The paper shredder let out a high-pitched whirring sound as he fed the papers through it.

He looked up, not smiling, but feeling a lightness and peace he hadn't felt in what seemed like years.

The day is coming. There will be reconciliation. I will take her back.

He walked back to his desk and raised the picture of his wife to his lips, kissing it tenderly.

"I'll see you again soon," he whispered as Bach's music filled the room.

Proper 13
Pentecost 11
Ordinary Time 18
Luke 12:13-21
by Argile Smith

Then What Will You Do?

Evan finally finished law school. The road to graduation for him had been paved with lots of ups and downs. Although his grades didn't show much promise, his lackluster academic record didn't pose as big a problem for him as his ego. His arrogance seemed to be his biggest flaw and it only got worse with each semester. Actually, Evan didn't register much concern about the way he barely passed his courses and warnings about his lack of potential for success didn't get much traction in his mind either. His dad had built a successful law firm in his hometown. Evan boasted more than once that his dad had an office for him once he graduated from law school. The certainty of the job waiting for him made him arrogant and careless.

Dr. McKenzie had watched Evan's bloated ego disfigure his perception of his future. He had enrolled in some of her classes, and she had tried to teach him but found herself getting frustrated with him. Evan's mammoth ego obstructed a clear picture of his foolish behavior.

Because Dr. McKenzie was a Christian, she noticed with concern an even more troublesome habit that plagued Evan. His arrogance about his place in his father's law firm had prevented him from factoring eternity into his life equation. She had heard him pontificate in class on the need to embrace life's adventures here and now with no thought of tomorrow. After all, he kept on insisting, we have the greatest fun when we live in the moment. He ignored serious consideration of his future.

On graduation day, Dr. McKenzie made her way to Evan at the reception so she could talk with him one more time before he left for good. She struck up a conversation with him by asking, "Well, Evan, now that you have finished law school, what's next?"

Evan replied with characteristic bravado, "Don't you remember? I'm going back home!"

"Then what will you do?" she asked him.

"Well," he said, seeing that he had an interested audience, "my dad's already got an office just waiting for me at his law firm. For as long as I can remember, he's told me that one day I would work with him. So now I am going to make his dream come true."

"Then what will you do?"

"My plan is to get my license, settle in my office, and work with my dad on a few cases to get a feel for it."

"Then what will you do?"

"I really haven't given it much thought. I've kicked around the idea of settling down, maybe getting married, buying a house. Things like that."

"Then what will you do"

"Oh, you know, have kids, take over the firm when Dad retires, maybe buy a boat."

"Then what will you do?"

"Doc, I can't really say that I've thought that far in advance. Maybe I'll give the firm to one of my kids and retire myself when I've got all I want."

Sensing that she was about to reach the end of Evan's patience, she asked, "Well, then what will you do?"

With her question, Evan let his frustration show with his reply. "I suppose I'll die like everybody else!"

Then she asked, "Then what will you do?"

In the parable of the rich farmer, Jesus showed the foolishness of failing to factor in eternity when we think about our future. So did Dr. McKenzie's conversation with Evan.

Proper 14
Pentecost 12
Ordinary Time 19
Isaiah 1:1, 10-20
by C. David McKirachan

Is Anybody Listening?

I volunteered as a guide for canoe trips down the Delaware River. That statement in itself is a story. It's enough to say that I was pastor of an inner-city parish at the time. I needed this like a sail needs wind. Johnsonburg Camp, in the wilderness of New Jersey (stop laughing), is a place of forests and holy connections. It drew me. I ended up on the board of trustees, but that's another story as well.

The canoe trips started at the camp with training and group-building, then we went by truck north into New York state to put in. Twelve senior high students and two counselors, 95 miles in five days — everything we used, including food, tents, sleeping bags, and frisbees, went into seven canoes. Canoeing is not what we were there to do. We were building and opening and expanding people — senior high students and decrepit old dudes as well. But with its demands and its joys and its thrills, the trip was a fitting context for growth. You learn a lot fast while negotiating whitewater or cooking meals when you'd rather lay down in the dirt and sleep.

There were always one or two who saw themselves as better than anybody else and set out to prove it. They were used to being large and in charge, or smart and capable, or all of the above. But a good amount of negotiating a river is counterintuitive. It's not something you can bully your way through, no matter how that has worked in other contexts. Experience is a great teacher. Listening to those who have an intimate knowledge of the river also works. Sometimes people prefer pain and humiliation to humility.

Two such lessons have to do with paddling faster than the current to allow steerage, and moving the back end of the canoe to let the current lever you off of rocks you may encounter. Both acknowledge that your strength is not as great as the river's. Both demonstrate that the water can be an ally, if you let it. And both demonstrate that what has always worked for you in other contexts may get you in trouble. "We always did it that way before" are very dangerous words.

Two characters inhabited what we called the NASCAR canoe, running ahead and proving that they were cool and powerful at every opportunity. They had inside jokes that they threw at the "pokes" and the "slugs." They were not allowed to get out of sight of the rest of us, but they flirted with this distance. Halfway through the morning they got to a nice set of rapids. They decided to demonstrate that the caution we exercised wasn't necessary if you were as cool as they were. In the middle of the whitewater was a good-sized rock dividing the flow. They decided in their testosterone-polluted minds to get there, climb out, and give commentary on our sad lack of skill as we went by.

By the time I realized what they were doing, they were backpaddling and slowing down — and then they landed broadside against the rock. NASCAR started filling with water. Rather than pushing the rear end around, they tried pushing off of the rock against the current. I went to the shore and jumped into the water above them. I could hear the aluminum screaming as it bent and the rivets popping like demonic corn. They climbed up on the rock and watched as the river wrapped the canoe around the obstruction like a shawl. Their equipment and packs and food took off downriver.

There was no need to chastise them. They'd been humiliated quickly and effectively. Whatever edge they thought they had on the group was gone and now they were in need. How far they had fallen.

We found most of their stuff along the way. But that night they slept on a tarp, while their sleeping bags hung in a tree drying. We had another canoe by the end of the next day. They'd been passengers for a while. Their racing days were over. By the end of the trip they began to laugh at themselves, a sure sign of health.

If only they'd listened. But maybe they needed the lesson. It's a terrible way to learn, but you know how pride is. It takes us places we never should have gone, invites us to do things others warn us about, and helps us to conveniently forget all the good advice wiser folk have offered. It reassures us that if we go through the motions of being nice people, we'll be fine. It leads nations to war. It invites us to forget about the poor, to forget about the ones who live in the margins, in the shadows. Isaiah knew. He understood the power of the river… and he understood the cost of forgetting.

Proper 15
Pentecost 13
Ordinary Time 20
Isaiah 5:1-7
by Stan Purdum

Donnie's Plant

My beloved had a vineyard on a very fertile hill. He dug it and cleared it of stones, and planted it with choice vines; he built a watchtower in the midst of it, and hewed out a wine vat in it; he expected it to yield grapes, but it yielded wild grapes.
— Isaiah 5:1-2

Although Lester was ninety years old, his health was still good and he was still able to take care of himself. He missed Sarah, of course, with whom he'd spent nearly 68 years, but he'd seen no reason to give up their apartment after she passed away the previous summer.

The only thing was, Sarah had been the outgoing one. She'd been the one who visited with their neighbors, chatted with the mail carrier, and made small talk with the children in the building. Lester wasn't unfriendly and he'd always said hello when he passed others in the complex, but he'd left the real socializing to Sarah. But now, with Sarah gone, Lester missed the human connection.

And so it was that he began to make an effort to be more talkative — and to his surprise, it wasn't as hard as he expected it to be. He became better acquainted with the folks on his floor and especially with the father and daughter who lived next door.

The father, a man in his thirties, was named Don, and his daughter, age nine, was Donnie. It had not always been just the two of them, but two years previously, Donnie's mother had been killed in an auto accident. So now the sad-eyed man and his bright-faced little girl were alone. Lester was never quite sure how much to say to Don, but Donnie made talking to her easy; she simply started conversations with Lester every time she saw him, and Lester made it a point to stop and speak back to her on each occasion. So eventually, the old man and the little girl began to think of themselves as friends.

Thus, it was not altogether surprising when one day in early summer Donnie came to Lester's door with a request. She was leaving the next day for a ten-day vacation with her daddy. Would Lester be willing to tend her plant while she was away? With little thought and without seeing the vegetation in question, Lester immediately agreed.

At daybreak the following morning, Don and Donnie started on their trip. Later in the morning, Lester stepped outside his door and found a child's small sand pail filled with nondescript dirt. Growing from this soil, but not thriving, was a fragile tree-like seedling. Competing with it for survival — and clearly winning — was a long reedy plant of some sort.

At that moment, Lester was struck by the enormity — and perhaps the foolhardiness — of what he had promised. A city dweller all his life, he'd never had a garden, and neither had he ever nurtured potted flora. But he *had* promised, and so, as he picked up the bucket, he uttered a prayer that Donnie's plant would not die on his watch.

A short time later, Lester told another neighbor about his dilemma and showed him the sand-pail planter. This man quickly identified the smaller plant as a maple tree seedling and the reedy stem as an obnoxious weed. This neighbor then invited Lester into his apartment and showed him his two dwarfed trees growing in pots. Learning of the special soil and nutrients this man used for his plants, Lester decided a trip to the local nursery was in order.

It was Saturday, and the large nursery Lester found was crowded and busy. After searching in vain for several minutes for a nursery worker to help him, Lester noticed a woman pushing a dolly loaded with shrubs. When he approached her, however, she indicated that she was a customer herself. But as Lester turned to walk away, he heard an inner voice say, "Turn back; this woman will help you."

So Lester obeyed. He changed direction and this time he told the woman he thought God had directed him to her for help. Who knows what the woman thought about that, but she politely stopped and gave him her attention. Lester introduced himself and told his story, and when he was done the woman, who introduced herself as Debbie, said that yes, she would help him. She left her dolly where it was and led Lester with his cart to various stops around the store until he had everything he needed to give the tiny tree a fighting chance — potting soil, fertilizer, plant food, and a larger pot. She then went back to her own shopping.

Lester slowly made his way to the checkout line, and when he arrived, he found himself in line behind Debbie. As they chatted casually, it must have become clear to her that Lester was still feeling out of his depth. She told Lester that she operated a small flower business herself. And then she said that if he would bring his supplies and the sand pail over to her shop that afternoon, she would handle the transplanting for him. With great relief, Lester said he would.

When Lester got to Debbie's shop that afternoon, Debbie immediately took charge, expertly separating the seedling from the weed and bedding it firmly in good soil in Lester's new roomy pot. Then, picking up the other plant, she said, "This is only a weed; we'll just throw it away."

"We can't do that," Lester said. "Donnie thinks that is part of the plant."

Debbie thought for a second and then said, "I know what. We'll replant it in the pail." She dumped out the original dirt, filled the little bucket with potting soil, and placed the weed in its new home. Before Lester left, she gave him specific instructions on how to care for both of his botanical charges.

For the remaining time Don and Donnie were away, Lester followed Debbie's instructions to the letter.

Thus, when dad and daughter came home, the little girl was thrilled to find her tiny maple tree flourishing, and the weed looking robust as well.

The next day, Lester heard a knock at his door. When he opened it, he found Donnie standing there beaming. In her hand was the sand pail containing the weed. "Thank you for taking care of my plant, Lester," she said. Then with both hands she extended the pail with its thriving weed and said, "This is for you."

As Lester accepted her offering, he told Donnie that he couldn't think of a nicer gift, and he thanked her for being so generous.

After she left, Lester realized that what he had told the little girl wasn't just a matter of politeness — he *couldn't* think of a nicer gift.

Proper 16
Pentecost 14
Ordinary Time 21
Jeremiah 1:4-10
by Rick McCracken-Bennett

God Searches for a Spokesperson

> *[The Lord said,] "Before I formed you in the womb I knew you, and before you were born I consecrated you; I appointed you a prophet to the nations." Then I said, "Ah, Lord God! Truly I do not know how to speak, for I am only a boy." But the Lord said to me, "Do not say, 'I am only a boy'; for you shall go to all to whom I send you, and you shall speak whatever I command you..."*
> — Jeremiah 1:5-7

So God says to this guy, "I need your help. The people aren't listening to me — again! I need someone who will speak for me and show them where they've gone astray. I need someone to call them back to me. It doesn't pay much, but you'd really be helping me out. What do you say?"

But the man says, "I wouldn't know what to say."

"Not a problem," says God. "I'll give you words. I'm just about done with the script now."

But the man says, "Oh God, I'd love to help, but I am an old man. I think I'll pass."

And God lets out a big, long sigh and goes in search of someone who can speak the truth to his people.

So God says to this middle-aged man, "I need your help. The people aren't listening to me — again! I need someone who will speak for me and show them where they've gone astray. I need someone to call them back to me. It doesn't pay much, but you'd really be helping me out. What do you say?"

But the middle-aged man says, "I wouldn't have any idea what I would say."

And God says, "Not a problem. I'll give you words to say. I'm finishing up the script as we speak."

But the man says, "Oh, I'd love to help, I really would. But I've got a job and a wife and kids. I'm afraid I'm going to have to pass."

So God lets out another big, long sigh and continues his search for someone to speak the truth to his people.

God comes upon a young man, fresh out of college. "I need your help. The people aren't listening to me — again! I need someone who will speak for me and show them where they've gone astray. I need someone to call them back to me. It doesn't pay much, but you'd really be helping me out. What do you say?"

And the young man says, "I took painting as my fine arts credit instead of public speaking. I wouldn't know what to say or how to say it."

And God says, "It really won't be a problem. I'm working on the script and you'll get a copy of it in plenty of time. All you'll have to do is read it."

But the man says, "I'd love to help, seeing that I'm young and an idealist and want to change the world, but I've got to get a real job so that I can pay off my student loans first. I'll have to pass."

God sighs a little longer and louder now, and continues his search for someone — anyone — who will speak the truth to his people.

So God says to this teenager, "I need your help. The people aren't listening to me — again! I need someone who will speak for me and show them where they've gone astray. I need someone to call them back to me. It doesn't pay much, but you'd really be helping me out. What do you say?"

And the teenager pulls his iPod earbuds out of his ears and says, "Huh?"

"I said, I need your help speaking to all the people of the world since they stopped listening to me."

And the teen says, "Like… well, you know, I like wouldn't know what to say, man."

And God says, "Not a problem. I'll give you all the words you need to say. I'll even read the script into a podcast, and you can listen to it and just tell them what I want them to hear."

And the teen says, "Dude, I would like to help, but man, like I've got to hang out with my friends and stuff. Be cool… I'll pass."

So God tries one more time. He comes upon a young boy, hardly twelve years old, and says to this child, "I need your help. The people aren't listening to me — again! I need someone who will speak for me and show them where they've gone astray. I need someone to call them back to me. It doesn't pay much, but you'd really be helping me out. What do you say?"

And the child says, "But I'm just a kid. I wouldn't know what to say."

And God says, "Look, I'll write it down. I'll give you the words. Don't worry."

And the child says, "Sure… okay!"

Which just goes to remind us to never ask a man to do a child's job.

Proper 17
Pentecost 15
Ordinary Time 22
Jeremiah 2:4-13
by Peter Andrew Smith

Thirsty for Living Water

"That's our church." Jim pointed at a large white building with a tall steeple along the street they were walking.

"Wow, that must be a beautiful place to worship," Sam said as they continued past stores and offices. "Who is your pastor?"

"Um. Tall fellow. Pretty good speaker. I think his name is DeSoya or DeSalle something like that." Jim paused in front of the church to squint at the sign. "Oh Desilvo. That's right, that's his name."

Sam chuckled as they resumed their walk. "I guess you don't get to Sunday service very often."

"We went regularly when the kids were in Sunday school. When Mary got sick I was there every week." Jim shrugged. "Since then I guess we got busy. You know with the girls moving out on their own we like to take advantage of the weekends."

"How long has it been since Mary finished chemo?"

"Seven years last March," Jim said. "That was a scary time let me tell you."

Sam patted him on the shoulder. "But you got through it."

"We did." Jim rubbed his eyes. "It was amazing how many people helped. It seemed like everyone I met on the street asked about her and told me they were praying for us. Good people in this town, you know."

Sam smiled. "Sure seems like a great place to live and raise a family."

"The absolute best place," Jim said. "It has been a great place to retire too — you saw the golf course."

They walked in silence for a few moments enjoying the sights of the small town.

"So why are you so unhappy?" Sam asked.

"What do you mean? Life couldn't be better for Mary and me. We've got time, good pensions, and we're both in good health. We're on top of the world."

Sam stopped and looked him up and down. "So why are you so unsettled?"

"Why do you mean?"

"Since Patty and I arrived, I've watched you do everything and nothing. You're up and down and down and up and can't stay still. You were always on the go but now you seem uncomfortable in your own skin."

"Huh." Jim shifted his weight from side to side. "I guess retirement isn't what I expected."

"How so?"

"Something's missing and I can't figure it out. I should be content and satisfied. I've got everything I always worked for but it isn't enough."

"Things okay with Mary?"

"Couldn't be better. Retirement lets us spent time together like before the girls were born."

"The girls doing okay?"

"Better than we imagined. Sally is happily married and expecting her first child and Suzy is setting the world on fire with her job. They both are happy and we couldn't be prouder."

"So what's wrong?"

"I don't know." Jim scratched his head. "Everything is good. Mary's good. The girls are good."

"You miss work?"

Jim laughed. "Not in the least. I love being able to do what I want with my days. We've taken some trips and I've been spending some time painting. But I can't shake the feeling that something is missing in my life."

Sam turned to look back at the way they had come. "Do you think it might be God?"

"What do you mean? I still believe in God."

"I never said you didn't. But how long has it been since you went to church, read your Bible, or prayed? When did you last make time for God in your life?"

Jim blew out his breath. "I guess it's been a while."

"You used to tell me how important it was for you and how you didn't feel the week was right unless you went to church on Sunday."

"Yeah, I always felt something, a peace and certainty, when I went to church." Jim paused and rubbed his chin. "Well, what I felt is hard to put into words and explain."

"Is it hard to explain in the same way as what you feel is missing in your life now?"

Jim nodded and they walked in silence for a few more minutes.

"You and Patty staying until Monday?" Jim asked.

"That's the plan."

"What are you doing Sunday morning?"

"Why?" Sam said. "You have a suggestion about what we could do?"

Jim smiled. "I think I would like to go to church."

Proper 18
Pentecost 16
Ordinary Time 23
Philemon 1-21
by Scott Dalgarno

Terminally Shy

The irony of the thing, of course, was how much Ben's mother always hoped he'd find a nice girl. Right up to the day he turned fifty she continued to tell him about "that nice Anderson girl who works at the bank."

"She's hardly a girl, Mother," he'd say. "She's worked at the downtown branch since I was in college." Ben's mother just didn't know what to make of her son. She'd tell her bridge-playing friends he was just "terminally shy." It took a real terminal diagnosis for things to really break for him, romantically speaking.

Well, it wasn't the cancer that did it. He'd met Suzanne a couple of months before the results from the MRI came back. She was new in Providence and began attending the Quaker meeting as a way of getting to know some people. Funny, a woman choosing a group that sometimes sits in a room for an entire hour saying nothing at all as a vehicle for finding community. If Ben was terminally shy, Suzanne's timidity was awaiting a serious prognosis.

Up until she met Ben, Suzanne told friends she was a cat person. That's all she'd say when a friend would ask if she wanted to meet a certain single friend or cousin. Suzanne had no problems with stray kittens (she often had two or three around her apartment), but she said she had no interest in making a project of someone's alcoholic brother.

Ben never was that specific about relationships. He'd just say in a general way, "Women are like elephants to me.

I like to look at them, but I'd never want to own one." His childhood friends thought him funny — funny ha-ha... and just plain, you know, funny. They'd long given up trying to interest him in a blind date.

What was truly funny, looking back, was that they met not within the walls of the church they both attended but in a pew in civil court. Alice, a mutual Quaker friend, was divorcing her husband of ten years, and she had enlisted both Suzanne and Ben to testify that she was a good mother and not the wicked witch her soon-to-be ex was trying to paint her as. Blessedly, neither was asked to take the stand, but the proceedings lasted an entire day and the two found themselves sharing a tuna sandwich alone in the funky cafeteria the county had been running for a hundred years. Ben had forgotten his wallet and Suzanne insisted the sandwich was much too big for her to eat alone.

There they sat in silence, elbows on formica, until Ben said it sounded an awful lot like church. Suzanne nearly choked and following that respectful silence it seemed neither shut up for a moment until the tumor on his brain took Ben's ability to speak away for good.

"For good" — where in the world did that term ever come from? The only good in it was that Ben, who was so wonderful at making faces anyway, used every muscle in his body to tell Suzanne how much he loved her once he couldn't say those words anymore.

The oddness of the fact that neither could say they'd ever had a boyfriend or girlfriend for their first five decades of life was balanced by the rapid progress of their courtship — a good word for love that began in a courthouse. The day Ben got his diagnosis, Suzanne brought him home. The cats already loved him — especially his massive chest and soft stomach. It was Linda, Ben's mother, who was troubled.

Here, all she seemed to crave, even in her widowhood, was a suitable companion for her son — and now that he'd found one she felt wretched about it every hour of every day. "What was he thinking?" she wondered. "What kind of hussy is this woman who's kidnapped my only son?" Linda was beside herself. And who heard all about it twelve times a day? Ben's sister Karen, of course.

Karen did what she'd done all her life — just look her mom in the eye and nod. That was her job; that was always her default position on everything when it came to family. Her mother had always been very good to her and the unspoken bargain was that Karen would just go along with whatever her mother had in mind. Now all she heard over and over was "How in the world could your brother do this to me, to us, to this family?"

And all the time Karen was just so happy that Ben had found anyone at all. Here he had brain cancer and yet she'd never seen him so happy in her life. There was a quietness about him now, a serenity that no member of her family had ever exhibited before. The Reasoners (oddly named) were never known for placid calmness. It was like Ben had become a wise teacher or something, and it was like it had happened overnight — or at least it seemed like that. There was just something about the combination of a life-threatening illness and a first love that put him in this holy zone... and Karen's mother couldn't see it. It was like she thought Ben had just been taken hostage by the Scientologists.

One day at the dollar store Karen finally had enough of her mother running down her brother. He'd been hospitalized that week, and Linda had not shown any interest in going to see her son.

"Mother," said Karen, adopting a tone Linda had never before heard on Karen's lips, "Ben is happy. Doesn't that mean anything to you?"

Stunned, Ben's mother began to repeat what a betrayal this relationship was to the whole family.

"Mother," said Karen, "let me finish."

"But you asked me a question," said Linda.

Karen continued right on. "Mother, after 48 years it's my turn to talk." Linda quieted right down.

"Mother, when John and I divorced last year you were a brick. You stood by me as closely as any daughter could hope for. My friends all commented on it. They thought you were amazing, the way you supported me but never interfered. Angie said over and over she wished she had a mother like you. All my friends just thought you were a breath of fresh air when it came to a family crisis."

Linda opened her mouth to speak.

"Don't you dare say a word," said Karen. "It's taken everything in me to get this far with you."

Linda hushed up.

"Oh, Mother, I'm sorry, but with Ben so sick and so in love, and Suzanne such a tender support — Mother, I just don't even recognize you anymore. You won't even go see him. Mother, you haven't even spoken to him in a week."

"How do you know th…"

"Because he told me. It was like the last thing he was able to say."

Linda began to weep silently.

"Ben's hurt, Mom. He doesn't know how long he's got, and he can't bear that this short time is being eaten up by this bitterness in your heart. I don't know if you're jealous or just afraid of the scandal this might cause with your friends. Frankly, I don't care. All I care about is Ben — and Mother, don't you think it's a good thing that after all these decades he's finally, you know, a little bit happy?"

Karen took a breath there in the aisle by the cards, where they were looking for something for her mom's sister Ada, who was about to turn eighty.

"Mom, Ben wishes he could have met Suzanne thirty years ago. He's sorry. I know he's sorry the relationship isn't more, you know, conventional. But he doesn't know what he could say to you if he could speak. You have to be the one to open the door. And don't think we have all the time in the world. All I know is, well, the oncologist says that with this kind of tumor..."

Linda shuddered.

"With this kind of tumor, anything can happen at any time." That was all Karen could say. They went out to the car and headed home.

Halfway to Karen's, Linda said, "Take me to the hospital." Karen obliged her mother. They drove in silence. Under the entrance, Linda asked if she could go in alone.

"Of course, Mother," said Karen. Linda walked slowly, breathing a bit hard, all the way to Oncology. Though she had not been there, she knew the room number — 413.

The door was open, but only halfway. It took everything in her to open it wide enough to enter. The lights were dim and a curtain was drawn around the bed. Linda paused. She heard nothing — no sound at all.

The silence terrified her. It made her fear the worst. Summoning all the courage she could, she looked around the curtain. There she saw her Ben, asleep in the recliner, wearing his hospital issue blues. Suzanne was there too, asleep in the hospital bed. The bed and recliner were pushed together. There they lay, holding hands.

It struck Linda that she had never seen a more beautiful couple in her entire life.

Proper 19
Pentecost 17
Ordinary Time 24
1 Timothy 1:12-17
by John Sumwalt

The Biggest Sinner

The saying is sure and worthy of full acceptance, that Christ Jesus came into the world to save sinners — of whom I am the foremost.   — 1 Timothy 1:15

A handsome, clean-cut young man sat in the visiting room of the county jail one day looking out through the bars, waiting for his appointment with the volunteer chaplain from one of the area churches. He was dressed in an orange jumpsuit; his hair looked like he had just gotten out of bed, which he had, if you can call a thin mattress on a cement slab a bed. When the deputies arrested him three days earlier, in the hallway outside of the classroom where he taught science at the local high school, he had been wearing a blue dress shirt, a brown paisley tie that matched his penny loafers, and tan slacks. His hair had been neatly combed and there had still been a hint of the Old Spice aftershave that he had splashed on his face just before leaving for school.

He sat there thinking about the fourteen-year-old freshman boy he had befriended, and what everyone would think when the story hit the newspapers. Sexual molestation charges against a teacher were always big news. He knew he would never teach again and that going to the state penitentiary for twenty or thirty years was a good possibility. There was a knot in the pit of his stomach that had not left from the moment the handcuffs were clapped on his wrists.

Pastor Jack Pearson, tall, thin, a little past middle age, with patches of gray in his beard that matched his wrinkled gray pastor's suit, made his way slowly up the steps to the county correctional facility. It just happened that he was on call, filling in for another pastor whose husband had been in an auto accident. As he stepped off the elevator he caught a glimpse of the young prisoner's profile across the lobby through the visiting room window. Suddenly he was filled with a deep, almost debilitating dread. He didn't know this young man, but he reminded him of someone he had pushed out of his memory for years and years.

It had only happened once and he had never done it again, but the reality that he had once molested a young boy came rushing into his consciousness. No wonder he had not wanted to come when he got the call. No one had ever found out about what he had done, but he had always lived with the fear that one day that boy, who would now be about the same age as the young prisoner in the orange jumpsuit, would come forward and identify him. The pastor was hit with the startling realization that this could and should have been him and that he had deserved the same fate and until now had somehow escaped even his own self-condemnation.

What would he say to this mirror image of his younger, darker self? What right did he have to pray and offer comfort and hope in the name of Christ when he carried the same stain on his soul? He whispered a prayer, "Oh God, help me," as he slowly opened the door to the visitation room. And before he introduced himself or offered his hand, he sat down at the table, looked straight into the young man's eyes, and said, "I have been where you are now, and I don't know what to say to you except that I believe in the mercy that Jesus offers to each one of us. I have experienced some of his grace, though I certainly never deserved it, and I know that if Jesus can forgive me and love me after what I did, he can and will forgive you too." Then he reached out and took the young man's hand and the two of them wept together.

Proper 20
Pentecost 18
Ordinary Time 25
1 Timothy 2:1-7
by C. David McKirachan

Hero

His name is John. His last name settles the issue of ancestry. It has double o's and is pronounced like there's only one. No question, Dutch. He's a chaplain in Seabrook Village, a full-service condo city near us. He also attends our ministers' lectionary study every Thursday.

Big and lanky, full of strength and self-deprecating humor, he's a nice guy to have around. He was an Army chaplain. After he'd been with us a while we started to hear stories about Vietnam. Like most combat veterans, his stories are terse, leaving out horrors, leaving out blow-by-blows. None of that would make any sense to those of us who have never faced enemies whose express purpose in life was to take ours.

He told us one story about sleeping in the building or tent where they did chapel. He'd put his cot up against boxes of Bibles. Just like everything in the Army, they come by the pallet load when they come. So he built room dividers out of them and had a little privacy in the midst of one of the most unprivate environments imaginable.

The mortar attack came when he was sleeping. Shells were lobbed into the camp over all the barbed wire and claymores and machine guns that defended the perimeter so carefully. No specific target or agenda, only to disrupt and frighten and if lucky to maim or kill someone who was close to the explosion. Shrapnel, bits and pieces of superheated metal, made sure the kill radius went a lot further than the explosive concussion. This particular shell landed close, he didn't say how close, but close enough to send fragments tearing toward him, sleeping. He never would have known. After the attack was over and clean up commenced, he found furrows torn in the crates of Bibles, pages ripped. The Word of God had defended him. He kept one of the Bibles, torn and mutilated. He showed it to us. He told us, chuckling, that it made a great illustration. In my book, he's a hero.

But this isn't about Vietnam. This is about a bumper sticker he has on his compact car. It's not the kind of sticker you'd expect from a combat veteran who'd seen the worst an enemy could do. He told us he likes to go the PX at the local Army base and park his car in the row with all the others, most of which proclaim with their bumpers, "God Bless America." Bunting and flags and patriotic decoration continue the push. His sticker has no stars or stripes. It says very simply, "God Bless Everybody, No Exceptions."

Like I said, this guy's a hero.

Proper 21
Pentecost 19
Ordinary Time 26
Psalm 91:1-6, 14-16
by Rick McCracken-Bennett

Be Not Afraid

"You shall not be afraid of any terror by night, nor of the arrow that flies by day; Of the plague that stalks in the darkness, nor of the sickness that lays waste at mid-day."
(translation from *The Book of Common Prayer*, 1979)

I'm not sure where I first heard it, but I was told that the #1 most requested song by our military men and women at worship services in Iraq is the Bob Dufford composition, "Be Not Afraid." That didn't surprise me. With words like, *be not afraid* and lyrics that speak of *crossing deserts* and *passing through raging waters* and *walking amid burning flames* and *standing before the powers of hell* it's difficult to think of a song that would speak more directly to the danger our men and women face every day in their service to our country. Every time I hear the song, I get a vivid picture in my mind of a dusty tent chapel in the desert and our military singing the soothing words of promise.

It's a favorite of mine as well. During particularly tough days I'll make my way into church, pick up my guitar, and play it from memory. I find myself singing the song to myself as I drive to a hospital emergency room to comfort a family that has had the unthinkable happen to them. I sing it to myself whenever I forget, as I too often do, that God is with me, God goes on ahead of me, and that my God will give me rest. While I haven't had to worry too much about arrows that fly by day or plagues that stalk me in the darkness or sickness that lays waste at midday, we all see enough scary things in a single day to keep a horror novelist supplied with plot lines for life.

As I write this, these headlines are streaming into my computer from the internet:

> University Student Faces Terrorist Charges
> *Be not afraid*
> Lawmakers' plane evades ground fire in Iraq
> *Be not afraid*
> Four Ohio stores evacuated in bomb scare
> *Be not afraid*
> Warming could worsen inland storms
> *Be not afraid*
> Family buries second son killed in war
> *Be not afraid*
> Stoning death boys found guilty
> *Be not afraid*

There were more, and unfortunately, in the weeks since I wrote these words, hundreds of headlines just as frightening have been printed in the paper and read on the evening news. More than ever we need to hear the words of the song *be not afraid* and the even stronger words of the psalm, *you* shall not *be afraid.*

I'm not surprised that when I "googled" the words *be not afraid*, I got thousands of hits that included poems, songs, articles, books, and blogs, most of them reminding us to not be afraid for we have a God that is with us, goes ahead of us, protects us, and guides us.

Years ago, I began to practice a discipline that I learned from a book by Eugene Peterson. Peterson reminds us of the words of the young man in the tomb in Mark 16 that go something like this: "Don't be alarmed; you are looking for Jesus of Nazareth... he has been raised... he is not here... go and tell his disciples and Peter that he is going ahead of you to Galilee, there you will see him as he promised."

The discipline he suggests is that we paraphrase those words as we make our way toward what might be a difficult or dangerous situation. It might go something like this: "Do not be afraid. Christ is risen and has gone before me to room 736 at Community Hospital where he will meet me as he promised." My role then, after praying these words, is to pay attention when I arrive at my destination to what the risen Christ has been doing before I finally arrived. I find myself far less anxious about what I am to say or do and simply try to fall into step with the work that Christ is already doing in that place.

Then… for at least a while, I am able to not be afraid; of the terrors (or the terrorists) of the night, the arrows of the daytime, or the plagues that stalk in the darkness.

Proper 22
Pentecost 20
Ordinary Time 27
2 Timothy 1:1-14
by John Smylie

Caught Not Taught

I love the reference to Timothy's family. One can imagine Timothy sitting in his one-room home watching his grandmother pray. Perhaps as a child he heard the prayers not only of his grandmother but also of his mother as they prayed for him, for members of their community, for folks in their family and for the world. If Timothy was like every other little boy when he was growing up, out playing with his friends and then coming home after doing a few chores and perhaps making a bit of income for the family, one can imagine that coming home for him was like coming into holy space. His home was filled with an invitation to the almighty God to be present.

Perhaps for Timothy, faith was caught not taught. I suspect, as a young child, he did spend some time in study with his elders but I suspect even more their faith, the faith of his grandmother and mother was an ever-present and shining example to him. Something in them attracted him, and one can only imagine that he wanted to have the light that he saw present in them in his own life.

When I first became interested in healing ministry, I heard about a healing mission coming to our home church. It was at a time in my life when I didn't spend a lot of time at church but I did believe that God was a God who was powerful. Sometimes churches to me did not seem like places where God was present but rather little communities that were caught up with the bitter struggles, petty infighting, and very often filled with mean-spirited people. Later I would learn that churches are hospitals for sinners, not museums for saints — so I suppose it was good that those folks with all their struggles allowed themselves to be under the influence of the good news of Jesus Christ.

In any case, I was excited by the neighborhood church offering a healing mission to the community. I decided I would go. The man who led the experience, the healing mission, was the international warden of the Healing Order of St. Luke the Physician. His name was John Park. I guess if I was to look at that language now — the warden — I might wonder if it was a prison ministry. In fact it was a ministry that sought to set people free from physical, emotional, mental, and spiritual ailments.

John looked like my image of a kung fu master. He had a bald head and a chiseled face. His spirit was soft and gentle and yet when he laid his hands upon anyone the power coming through them was strong and tangible. The strength of Christ within him contrasted against his own deeply humble spirit, and I found myself wanting to be like him. This was clearly an example of faith being caught not taught. Here in front of me was a man who believed in the power of God, and allowed himself to be a channel of the same. How blessed we are when we have examples in our life — people — who reflect to us the height and depth and breadth of God. How blessed we are when the sound teaching of our Lord is not only spoken but demonstrated by a life that is dedicated and possessed by the passion of Christ and the presence of the Holy Spirit.

How blessed we are when there are those around us who radiate the love of Christ — John Park was one of those teachers for me and I find myself still desiring to catch a hold of the goodness and power of the Lord that was so present within him. Sometimes we may not be aware of the gifts we have — particularly the gift of presence — the

Lord's presence within us. Pray that we will be faithful grandmothers and grandfathers, mothers and fathers, brothers and sisters, pray that we will all be faithful children of our Lord and reflections of the power and presence of Jesus Christ.

Proper 23
Pentecost 21
Ordinary Time 28
Luke 17:11-19
by Keith Hewitt

The Outsider

This was his favorite time of day. The sun was low, dipping behind the hills, and the sky was pearly gray, mottled with dark clouds, as though night had fled and left pieces of itself behind. He sat beneath a tree at the top of a hill and stared toward the horizon; letting the cool breeze wash away the worries of the day. Below, in the little pocket of a valley where the trail wound through, his companions were starting a fire and spreading blankets where they would sleep for the night.

Sure, there was always the chance of running into the occasional bandit, or bear, but he preferred sleeping out in the open, these nights, rather than in the smoky, stifling homes crammed together in the villages that marked the road between Galilee and Jerusalem. He let his head rest against the rough bark of the tree and breathed deeply of the cool, clean air.

Then a twig snapped and his eyes were suddenly open and alert, looking toward the sound. Almost instantly, they relaxed as they fell on the familiar form and face of the Teacher. He put one hand down next to himself, started to get up — stopped when the Teacher looked down at him and shook his head slightly. Instead, the Teacher sat down next to him and nodded toward the valley; he relaxed, and laid his head back again.

"So, Thomas — what happened today?" the Teacher asked, his voice gentle as his eyes.

Thomas turned his eyes toward the Teacher without moving his head, until he could see him out of the corners, looking almost sideways. He hesitated and then admitted frankly, "I don't know." Then he smiled, shrugged slightly. "But then, I often don't, until you've explained it to us."

"You're learning — you're all learning. But there is much to learn and little time."

Thomas frowned; he didn't like it when the Teacher spoke like that. As often as he was confused by what the man said, he was all too sure about what the Teacher meant when he talked about time being short... and it made him uncomfortable to know the *what* without understanding the *why* — if there was one.

"Do you understand leprosy?" the Teacher asked.

Thomas shrugged. "I don't know anyone who's had it, of course. But I know it's a sickness that attacks your body and makes you inhuman, unclean."

"It's more than just a painful, shameful sickness — it's more like a wall," the Teacher said, his face drawn down in a frown as he spoke. "It's a wall that's thrown up overnight, from the moment it's discovered, separating the leper from his family, from his home, and from his livelihood. When a man becomes a leper, he becomes unclean, and when he's unclean he's cut off from everything he ever held dear, from everything that *completed* him as a man. A man with leprosy is separated from who he could be, by what he's become."

Thomas nodded in the dim light. "It's a tragic illness."

"That's why the Samaritan was so full of praise when he returned. It was as though I had opened a gate through that wall by healing him — in any real sense of the word, I had given him his life back."

"I can see that," Thomas said slowly. "I think I understand. But then why did only the Samaritan return?"

It was the Teacher's turn to shrug. "Who can say?"

Thomas raised his head, then, and looked at him — smiled as he met his eyes. "Not I, Teacher — but I'm pretty sure *you* can."

The Teacher reflected his smile, nodded. "Perhaps it was because he was already an outsider, so he had a deeper appreciation of the pain of being apart from having a whole life. Or perhaps it was because he is not as closely tied to the priests of the Temple as the others and was willing to give thanks *outside* the walls of the Temple. Perhaps he recognized that he could give thanks to the Father through me and did not have to be in the Temple to do it."

Thomas studied the Teacher for a few moments — his expression was harder to see, now, in the gloom. "Teacher," he said slowly, "it is times like this that my head begins to hurt."

Another smile flickered in the shadows. "I'll leave you with this thought, then. Consider that sin is like leprosy — it disfigures men, makes them less than what they could be, and it cuts them off from the completeness of being in harmony with the Father. And now the Son of Man offers a chance to be cleansed, a chance to be healed — a way through the wall of sin, back into harmony with the Father, just as the leper who is cleansed of his disease can rejoin life."

The Teacher stood up, then, leaned down and stretched his hand to Thomas as he continued. "Like healing, forgiveness is there for anyone who has faith — perhaps it's right that an outsider should be the first to praise God for it. Perhaps it was easiest for *him* to recognize what it meant to have the chance to go home again."

He grasped Thomas' hand, pulled him up easily. They stood face-to-face for a moment, then, hands clasped — and it seemed to Thomas that the Teacher's grip held him tightly. "Know this, Thomas — I've come to take on their burdens and to share the gift of forgiveness with *all* men... but only those who are blessed with faith and truly understand their own nature, their own brokenness, will understand the power of forgiveness to make them whole, to bring them back to the Father again."

Thomas looked back at him steadily. "I think I understand."

The Teacher looked at him closely, nodded, and released his grip. "You begin to understand," he agreed, "but you have questions." Then he smiled. "With you, Thomas, there are always questions."

And so the two men continued to talk as they descended the hill, rejoining their companions in the valley.

Proper 24
Pentecost 22
Ordinary Time 29
Psalm 119:97-104
by C. David McKirachan

Deontologize the Principle of Parsimony

I had a hard time determining a major in college. I vacillated between History, Anthropology, English Lit., and Geology. I like field trips. There was one professor who fascinated me. He was older than the norm, played the cello, rode an ancient but shiny three-speed bike around the campus, enjoyed good sherry, chuckled around his pipe, and faced the tirades of adolescent arrogance with the aplomb of calm courage. His questions bothered me like fleas. I itched at them long after class. Dr. Strodach was a Philosophy professor. I took any class that had his name on it. I learned. He's why I majored in Philosophy. My father's Ph.D. from Princeton in Metaphysical Philosophy had absolutely nothing to do with it. Congenital disorders often go unnoticed.

Dr. Strodach gently goaded us toward a consideration of our own place in the world by inviting us to consider the monsters of the contemplative discipline. He refused to accept rote repetition of Plato. He wanted us to wrestle with the shadows on the wall of our own lives. What were our ideals? He poked holes in each and every balloon I lofted. And in the grand deflation, I discovered how the defense of my own foolishness limited my journey. He taught me not to tolerate fools. But he taught me how to have enough manners to not make myself one by considering myself far separated from their foolishness. This guy was the real deal. He reminded me of my father without all the Oedipal baggage.

In my senior year he got sick. Not the flu kind, the hospital surgery kind. We had just started a year-long trek through the metaphysicians. I was devastated. His replacement was a teacher who shall not be named here. The guy made me nuts. He loved to demonstrate his superior knowledge and use it like a lash to move us through the material. He was boring in lecture and did not deal well with questions no matter how insightful or desperate they were. The day we dealt with Occum's Razor was the final straw. This philosophic principle came from a Scottish monk, naturally. He said the simplest construction is best, the KISS principle comes from him. Keep it simple stupid. The not-so-esteemed professor held forth on the metaphysical chaos that swirls about our heads, calling forth Occum as the shining knight of logic to wield his razor in our defense. He then announced just what that razor was. "Deontologize the principle of parsimony." It was like getting a garbage compactor for a romantic gift (that's another story). It was like… This… boob (and that's generous) just cut himself with the razor he was showing us how to use. So much for keeping it simple.

In my stunned bewilderment, I suddenly heard Dr. Strodach chuckling. He never took his pipe out of his mouth. He just chuckled around it. I calmly held up my hand. Our ranting boob of a professor ground to a halt and glared at me. Raising his chin as to consider what kind of bug was presuming to disturb him, he pontificated, "Yes?" He made it a three-syllable word.

The bug humbly asked, "Sir, what does 'deontologize' mean?"

The boob stared at me, considering exactly what would be the best way to squash me. As realizing this gave him another moment to demonstrate his mental superiority, he launched into a tirade of multisyllabic balderdash. Finally considering me sufficiently squashed, he checked his notes and rebooted his destruction of Occum. I raised my hand again. He shuddered to another halt. He again addressed me with all the scorn of a Ph.D. to a fool. "Yes?" This time it was a four-syllable word.

The bug humbly begged, "Sir, what does 'parsimony' mean?"

Now to you this may not seem like a horribly offensive set of questions. You may have been wondering yourself. But to the class who had become numb under his lash it was clear there was a ray of Strodach sunshine beaming into our darkness. The boob stared at me for a good thirty seconds, looked at his notes, and dismissed the class.

Small victories mean a lot to slaves. We had to pass the class with a B if we were Philosophy majors. Small victory or not, we were still bugs in the amber of multisyllabic balderdash. I considered this as I plodded into the boob's room for the next class. I was waiting to pay for my small victory. I was late. The class was silent as I closed the door. I was afraid to turn around. As I came into the room, I saw Dr. Strodach sitting on the window sill smiling around his pipe. I was terrified that I would turn around and realize I was still in the boob's hell.

Dr. Strodach said to my back, "What's the matter Mr. McKirachan? I thought you believed in the resurrection of the body."

That good-humored master teacher gave me a gift, "sweeter than honey." He taught me the validity of grace under fire and demonstrated the courage to claim it. He also taught me that the truth will make us free.

God bless you, Dr. Strodach.

Proper 25
Pentecost 23
Ordinary Time 30
2 Timothy 4:6-8, 16-18
by Argile Smith

Looking Ahead

Jerry could hardly believe that he had been accepted! But, that's exactly what the dean of the university said in her letter to Jerry. Giddy with excitement, he held the letter in his hand and called Dawn, his wife of only a few months. She affirmed Jerry's dream of enrolling in graduate school. Now that he had been accepted, she favored the idea of uprooting themselves from North Carolina and moving to Los Angeles.

One other detail in the letter, however, caught Jerry and Dawn off guard. According to the dean, Jerry would be expected to enroll immediately for the next semester, which meant that he needed to relocate quickly. Jerry didn't really think that he would be accepted, so he hadn't done anything about getting ready to move.

Dawn insisted that he should go ahead to Los Angeles. She would stay in North Carolina and join him as soon as she could serve out her resignation notice at work, pack and load their belongings, and make the trek across the country. Reluctantly Jerry agreed and drove their "good" car to the place where his academic dream would come true, expecting Dawn to arrive shortly in a rented truck loaded with boxes and furniture.

For Jerry, the trip west went well. He made his way to the apartment complex where he and Dawn would make their new home without a problem. Getting from the new apartment to the university where he would study turned out to be easy too.

For Dawn, things didn't go so well. She had to go through the ordeal of packing up everything herself, and she had to handle her family's discomfort over her decision to drive across country alone. Of course, she also had to contend with her own fears about moving to a strange, new part of the world she had never visited before now.

Worst of all, she missed Jerry. Each day that passed since he left brought a new dimension to the pain she bore because she couldn't see him. As she came home from work every afternoon, her dread of nightfall became more difficult to bear. She and Jerry had always looked forward to that time of the day. At home after work, they had come to view nightfall as their time to be together, to revisit their dream for their future, to experiment with the new adventure of preparing dinner, and just to enjoy each other's company. That's why Dawn felt so sad when the sun set.

Of course, she and Jerry talked to each other all the time. Thanks to cell phones and the internet, they stayed in almost constant contact. They sent pictures to each other and corresponded on the moving details at every opportunity. Still, Dawn couldn't be with Jerry in person.

Finally, the day arrived for Dawn to hop in the truck and drive away from the home she had known for most of her life. Her parents noticed that she didn't seem to be sorrowful, but hopeful. When they asked her questions, she answered in ways that assured them of her eagerness to get on the road. When they brought up the new scenery, new opportunities, and new challenges of her new home, they asked her about what she looked forward to most of all once she reached her destination. Without batting an eye, she answered, "Seeing Jerry."

As Paul wrapped up his life, he told Timothy to look ahead. Living can be difficult, but Christians can look forward to seeing Jesus one day.

Reformation Day
Jeremiah 31:31-34
by Scott Dalgarno

A Change of Heart

Carol Lee and Jerry hadn't been married long. They had lots of love but little money. Living in the city they took what they could get: a one-bedroom, no-parking, apartment in a neighborhood where it was Halloween every day.

Sirens were ubiquitous and for every church there were six tattoo parlors. One of those was located right next door to their apartment house. Normally very accepting, Carol Lee was incensed by it. The place was busy until late every night. The people who showed up there were often loud, drunk, and even violent. Confrontations on the sidewalk in front of the place happened, it seemed, nightly. Carol Lee was livid. She'd walk all the way around the block to get to her apartment instead of taking a few steps to cross in front of the horrid shop.

"Come to bed," Jerry would insist, while Carol Lee would rip whoever she saw going in. This evening it looked like a single mother with two toddlers in tow. "That woman with the bleached blond hair obviously can't afford to feed her children and look, she's spending money on body art!"

When a man in their complex complained to the police about the noise, his Honda's tires were slashed. Things were getting bad. When Carol Lee brought up the parlor Jerry blew her off saying he wasn't getting involved and she better not either. His policy was simply, "Let's get the kind of jobs that'll pay us enough to get out of here." But Carol Lee couldn't think about that with little children suffering because of their mother's bad choices. She decided to do something that was entirely Carol Lee. She decided to get a tattoo.

Yep, she couldn't change them by hating them so she decided to get down and dirty with them. Maybe if she understood them better something would shift in her or maybe even in them. So, the question hung in the air: What kind of tattoo?

Carol Lee poured over books of quotations at the public library and settled on something by Madame de Stael. Armed with her choice, she showed up on the doorstep of the shop. She got there near noon when they opened. It was much too early for them to be busy. She'd found the walls of the place covered with pictures of naked women, knives and axes dripping blood, Nazi art, Our Lady of Guadalupe, the American flag in various positions, and human skulls.

Carl, the proprietor, was putting some Japanese lettering down a young woman's lovely neck. Carol Lee admitted to herself that it was tasteful if not beautiful.

Another artist, Enrique, asked if he could help her. "Yes," she said, "I want a tattoo. No art, just simple lettering to go around my left wrist."

"Saying what?"

She handed him the piece of torn notebook paper with the quote: "Who understands much, forgives much."

"Why this?" he asked.

Because I live next door and you guys scare me with your fighting and loud talk and scary customers," she said. "I want to understand you more so I can forgive you."

"Geez," said Enrique to Carl. "Dude, we got to stop fighting so much. We're scaring our neighbors."

Carl tried to downplay the problem but Carol Lee stopped him quickly, saying she wasn't there to complain. She just wanted to get a tattoo and get to know them a little bit while doing it.

That diffused everything. Carl smiled and Enrique laughed quietly and led Carol into the back where he opened a book of samples. He showed her a line from Hitler's Mein Kampf.

"No," said, Carol Lee, "I really want the quote about forgiveness."

Enrique really chuckled this time. "No," he said, "I'm not trying to get you to wear Nazi propaganda, but you still need to pick a writing design for me to copy."

Carol Lee laughed at her own ignorance. "Sure, sure, that's very nice. I'm sure it'd look less harsh in German."

In twenty minutes he was done and the words looked as delicate as her tiny wrist.

It seemed like overnight that Carl and Enrique became Carol Lee's best friends. She passed in front of their business many times every day now, waving and joking and showing everyone the lovely sentiment made even lovelier because she wore it with such pride.

The neighborhood changed too. No more fights broke out, and Enrique and Carl made sure the neighborhood was safe for all who lived there. Jerry and Carol would bring dinner down to the fellows and their families once a week or more. The bloody knives and swastikas disappeared from their walls and baskets of flowers now hung from the eaves of the business. People hardly recognized the place anymore. Police walked by now, shaking their heads.

All Saints Day
Daniel 7:1-3, 15-18
by Stan Purdum

Crazy Dreams

"Gee, Louise, you look pretty rough. And you're twenty minutes late, too." That was Alice's comment as her coworker finally got to her desk that Monday morning.

"I know," Louise said. "I didn't sleep very well again last night. And I decided to take the bus, and it was running a little behind."

"You rode the *bus*? How come? Your car in the shop?"

"No. I just thought it might be wise."

"You mean you're too sleepy to drive?"

"It's not that," Louise said, sighing. "You remember last week I told you I'd been having crazy dreams but couldn't remember what they were about when I woke up?"

"Sure."

"Well, for all three weekend nights, I've awakened remembering."

"This sounds *spooky*," Alice said with a shiver.

"Well, it sort of is. And it's why I had trouble going back to sleep."

"Tell me more."

"All my dreams are about cars. In one of Friday night's dreams, I was driving along a road to some place I wanted to go. I don't know where it was, but I was looking forward to getting there. But then I hit mud hole and got stuck. I couldn't get the car free."

"Well, that would be a problem, I guess, but it doesn't sound that scary."

"Except that the whole car started sinking into the mud hole, and I couldn't get out. The mud was just closing over the windows when I suddenly woke up."

"Oh. I see what you mean."

"Yes," said Louise, "but Saturday's dream was worse. I was driving a car in a race when the *steering wheel* came off in my hands. I couldn't get it back on and the car started careening all over the course. I woke up just before another car plowed into me."

"Ouch," said Alice.

"But last night's was worse yet. I was driving down a busy street with all three of my kids in the car, and suddenly, I drove over a cliff! I woke up as we were falling. I could even hear the kids screaming."

"Ah. So you took the bus because you are afraid all that stuff about cars was a warning about an accident or something next time you drove?"

"Yes. It makes sense, doesn't it?"

"I'm not so sure. Maybe you should talk to somebody who knows something about what dreams mean."

"You know somebody like that?"

"It happens that I do. He's a psych professor where my husband teaches. I bet he'd be willing to talk to you if you asked."

Louise considered Alice's suggestion and then said, "Maybe you're right. I don't want to keep putting in nights like these last ones. You have his number?"

A few days later, Louise and Alice were again talking in the office. Louise looked a lot better, and she had driven to work that morning.

"So what did Professor Benton say?" Alice asked.

"He said dreams are symbolic and that they usually aren't literally about the things in the dreams themselves. So he said that my dreams about the cars probably have nothing to do with automobiles or accidents but with something else altogether."

"Like what?"

"Like control. He said that if you dream of yourself in the driver's seat, you may mean that you see yourself as taking control of your life. But if, as in my dream, the car gets stuck in the mud, it may be symbolizing a feeling that I am are going nowhere, or that my life is in a rut."

"Does that fit you?"

"You bet."

"What about the crashes?"

"Yeah. That. Well, he said that dreaming that my car crashes could be my subconscious mind symbolizing that I feel my life is out of control."

"Wow. You look pretty calm for hearing all that."

"Well, I can't say it was good news," Louise said, "but it does fit how I've been feeling. And at least now I know I need to confront some stuff at home."

"So how'd you sleep last night?" Alice asked.

"Like a baby."

Proper 26
Pentecost 24
Ordinary Time 31
2 Thessalonians 1:1-4, 11-12
by Rick McCracken-Bennett

Small but Mighty Faithful

> ... [W]e ourselves boast of you among the churches of God for your steadfastness and faith during all your persecutions and the afflictions that you are enduring. — 2 Thessalonians 1:4

We all know of a congregation that is doing extraordinary work for the kingdom of God. Here is a story of one of them.

I often find myself speaking of a small church I once served. I had taken a ten-year hiatus from my work as a pastor and this was the church I served when I reentered.

I'll never forget the evening I met their Vestry and we hammered out an agreement that would amount to about a one third of my time spent in this small, rural, shrinking village. While the Vestry met to discuss whether or not to call me, I walked into the sanctuary and had a look around. My first thoughts bring me to shame upon remembering them. I stood in the pulpit and looked out at the smallest nave I had ever seen. Perhaps if you were careful you could squeeze a hundred in but sixty or seventy looked to be about the most it would hold. I remember thinking (I am ashamed to say) that I couldn't imagine preparing a sermon for only those few people. It was actually worse than that when I learned that only about forty folks showed up on any given Sunday.

But what was I to do? This would allow me to gradually get back into the active ministry while I kept my day job. It would work for now. It turns out that I stayed there joyfully for over eight years, the longest pastorate in the 100-year history of this church.

I, of course, quickly grew to love these people, their village, and the smell of the nave on Sunday before anyone else showed up. I preached, visited, married them, and buried them. It was a wonderful time in my life and the life of my family.

After I left, even though we had set up a cluster relationship to ease the financial burdens of this and two other churches, the congregation began to shrink from forty to less than 25 most times. And yet, they kept at it. Too proud to ask the diocese for money, they hunkered down and refused to give up. They looked the death of the congregation in the face and kept going with the mission and ministry of the church.

You see… this little church provided (at least) three essential ministries to that part of the county and no one in the congregation was willing to let those go.

Many years before, they had started a program that fed the elderly every weekday with a home-cooked meal, often with food from their own gardens, mixed with lots and lots of fun and fellowship. Though the program now received funding from outside the church, the congregational volunteers who work each and every day have kept this service available to the sixty or more people that showed up each day. I can't imagine that village without this program.

They also provided an "off-the grid" pantry. Though they understood why other pantries in the county could only allow a certain number of visits a month, this church decided to not link up with them and simply gave food to whoever came their way. That pantry continues solely on donations from the congregation and though they have no doubt been "taken" a time or two, they give gladly to the poor who come to their door week after week.

If that wasn't enough for a congregation of around 25 people, they provide a well-attended after-school tutoring program that, with the help of a small grant, allows them to have a certified teacher to lead their work.

Perhaps this doesn't sound like much. Certainly it pales in the sight of program- and corporate-sized churches and their work. But I wonder… what if every 25 people in our current congregations worked as faithfully in their mission and ministry? What would happen to the hunger, the illiteracy, and the loneliness in our parts of the mission field?

As you might imagine, I never tire of telling all I meet about this small but very faithful congregation. I never stop giving thanks to God for them.

Proper 27
Pentecost 25
Ordinary Time 32
Luke 20:27-38
by Frank Ramirez

The Wrong Lens

Four years and two years before he began kindergarten, our youngest son, Jacob, accompanied his older brother and sister to that special classroom. He was fascinated by the playground — especially the elephant slide. It was an ordinary enough slide but on the sides were painted elephants. Time and again he would ask if he could play on the elephant slide, but I always said no and that his time would come when it was his turn to go to school.

That made the approaching first day all the more exciting. As it grew nearer and nearer his excitement grew. Finally it came. He was dressed in a brand new outfit, with his equipment under his arm, but all of that was forgotten as he ran past the gate and into the play yard. Finally he would get a chance to play on the elephant slide. It was his turn.

As I parked he ran from the car into the playground, right up to the slide, and stopped short. I caught up. He had a stunned look on his face.

"What's wrong, Jacob?" I asked.

"Who shortened the slide?" he replied in alarm.

Nothing had changed. I took a look to make sure. Then it hit me. I was the same height then as I was the first day I brought his older brother to his first day. The slide looked the same to me.

But Jacob was four years older. And four years taller. The slide looked smaller to him!

I assured him that nothing had changed and the moment's suspicion gave way to a shrug and then a good ten minutes of fun on the slide before he was called in for the start of class.

* * *

The prophet Haggai did his best to inspire the people to rebuild the temple. The first temple had been destroyed by the Babylonians in 586 BC and many of the people had been taken away into exile. Now the Babylonians themselves had been conquered, and God's people had been sent home by the Persians, who encouraged their subject nations to retain their national identities, religions, and cultural practices — as long as they paid their taxes on time.

Sixteen years had passed since the return of the people, and there'd been problems with inertia, building permits, co-operation with the locals, and simply the great difficulties that went with getting resettled in a distant land. But finally building had begun.

Now those who had been children when the first temple was destroyed didn't think much of the second temple, and they said so, loudly. Haggai echoes their complaints when he asks, "Who is left among you that saw this house in its former glory? How does it look to you now? Is it not in your sight as nothing?" (Haggai 2:3).

But the reason it looked as nothing in their sight was they had seen the first temple as children — and it had looked huge. They had grown — not only in height, but in life experiences. They had endured two major disjunctures, the anguish that went with deportation and the joy of returning.

The present reality of the temple could not match their childhood memories. They were looking at the temple through the wrong lens, seeing the present reality but not perceiving it for what it was — and complaining loudly!

Haggai promised future prosperity and that "The latter splendor of this house shall be greater than the former..." (v. 9) but that promise could probably only come true when the naysayers and the complainers stepped aside. Just as Jacob had to accept the fact that the slide hadn't shrunk, but he had grown, so those in Haggai's day had to recognize they were quite as capable of matching the feat of building a magnificent temple, with God's help, as their ancestors. Indeed, though it took hundreds of years, the Great Temple of Jerusalem was, in Jesus' day, one of the great wonders of the world.

Looking through the wrong lens changes everything. When the Sadducees asked Jesus a question about a woman who married seven brothers, one after the other as she was widowed time and time again, they asked not as an academic exercise, nor as an honest debate about the meaning of scripture. They asked using the lens of skepticism — skepticism about the resurrection, skepticism about the scriptures, and especially skepticism about Jesus. They were incapable of recognizing that the Lord of Life, who would embody the resurrection, was in their midst.

We too must look at what God can accomplish in our midst but not through a lens that so glorifies the past that we discount the miracles of the present. It will do no good to adopt a pose of skepticism or despair. Trust and faith in God, and God's goodness will teach us that the present is good, despite what others tell us they see, and that the future will be glorious.

Proper 28
Pentecost 26
Ordinary Time 33
Luke 21:5-19; Isaiah 12
by Argile Smith

In That Day

Even though she had just turned her calendar to the month of October, the semester had already been too long for Kim. Her first semester at the university had been tough. The difficulties associated with adjusting to campus life, getting over syllabus shock, and learning how to sleep in a dorm paled in comparison to her almost constant ordeal with homesickness. At night, she would cry herself to sleep, thinking about her bed at home and her parents. She even missed her little brother, who had been nothing but a pest to her as far back as she could remember.

She could hardly wait for Thanksgiving break so she could return there for an entire week. That's why her heart sank to the floor when her mother called her to say that a trip for home at Thanksgiving wouldn't be possible. A strange and sudden change in plans at home left her with only one option: to drive up to her uncle's house for Thanksgiving Day. The rest of her time would be spent at school in the library or in front of her computer, and in either case, all by herself.

In her anger over what she considered to be unfair treatment, she emailed her mother about the change in plans and the devastation it had caused. First, Kim blamed her for being insensitive and thoughtless. She went on to remind her mother of the favored treatment her little brother had received all of his life, adding that he had been away at school, such a change in plans wouldn't have been considered at all!

Kim sent her searing message and sat there in her dorm room. The late afternoon sun cast a sad glow over her sullen face while tears of disappointment trickled down her cheek. She waited for a minute and wondered if she had done the right thing. After all, her mom couldn't do anything about the change of plans. Kim's dad wanted to visit his mother who had been sick for a long time. In fact, the doctors agreed that the past couple of birthdays had not been good to her frail frame and that no medicine could be prescribed that would stretch out her days. Kim's dad didn't want to live in regret over not making one last visit, and Kim's mom understood completely. That's why she made arrangements for Kim to spend Thanksgiving with her brother and his wife, Kim's favorite relatives.

But at the moment Kim didn't think about her dad's need to see his mother. She could only think about her agony over needing to see her folks and the home she missed so much.

Two hours passed before Kim got a reply from her mom. She wrote, "Sweet Kim, I knew that not being home at Thanksgiving would break your heart. I understand why you are mad at me. Keep in mind that Thanksgiving is just a few weeks away from the end of the semester. On that day, you can put your papers and exams behind you and come for a long Christmas break. It will make having to wait worthwhile. Keep thinking about that day, and it will help you to get through the days between now and then. And remember that no matter how you feel about me, I love you."

In time, Kim took her mother's advice to heart. She began to see every setting sun as a signal that she would have one less day to wait until she could go home.

Christ the King
Proper 29
Jeremiah 23:1-6
by C. David McKirachan

What's the Stick For?

When I started this job, over thirty years ago, I was amazed at people's intransigence. They didn't want to change, even when it made sense. I knew the new ideas made sense, because they made sense to me. God, I was young. "We never did it that way before" was their perfectly logical reason to keep doing things that were not only irrelevant and unnecessary but sometimes patently self-destructive. I used to grind my teeth and pound the pavement, trying to walk off the frustration.

I remember the first time someone set me up for the express purpose of hurting me and destroying the good the church was trying to do. It was like finding a pit dug in an interstate for no reason except to hurt and disrupt. It was a bloodless form of terrorism, right in my own backyard. It wounded my sense of hope. Working creatively for the kingdom had never been defensive for me. How could I trust? Some of the flock were carrying bombs.

It made me reconsider my attitude toward evil. It made me realize that part of my call was not only to take advantage of the church as a staging area for rescuing the lost but to also make sure that this sanctuary was really safe. Evil wasn't only out there. I remembered the Lord's words, "The Kingdom of God is *among*, or it could be *within* us." I had just discovered that the "dark side" was also *among* or it could be *within* us.

I had always been taught to be humble, non-judgmental, and, in a word, nice. I began considering the nature of the abuse that flourishes in a home where people try their best to be loving and end up enabling. Yes, the abusers are themselves victims, but being merely nice to them will not help them or their victims. People who were bent on exercising their muscles of domination and control in the church were suffering under burdens of anger and hurt. The best way I could minister to them was to confront their behavior and protect the family of faith.

I worked at Johnsonburg Camp as a volunteer. It's 400-odd acres of woods in northwestern New Jersey. On one hike I found a red cedar branch, heavy at one end, knotted and gnarled as cedar can be. I'd taken it and worked with it, hand and pocket knife, until it became a smooth staff, too heavy for a walking stick. I put it in the corner of my office at the church. It reminded me of my responsibility as a pastor. We're here to care for the flock. We keep them together. We scope out new pastures and good water. We help them lamb and keep them healthy and out of holes. We also keep the predators away. Wolves aren't sheep. That's one reason shepherds carry a big stick.

But the staff is also there to remind me that the evil I have to watch for is not only out there somewhere — it is also within. It is as close as a budget meeting or a ladies' circle. It is as close as my own arrogance and self-righteousness. Woe to us if we forget. We'll be on the menu.

Thanksgiving Day
John 6:25-35
by Keith Hewitt

Bread

She was sitting at the kitchen table when her son returned with a jarring door slam and a triumphant, "I'm back!"

She leaned to her right so she could peek out toward the living room where he was busily shedding his Evil Jester costume. A navy blue pillow case sat on the floor next to him, bulging with treats. "Did you have fun?"

"Yeah! We went farther tonight than last year — all the way down to the tracks and back. Katy's dad jumped out of the bushes down on Harding in a Grim Reaper costume and chased us for two blocks." He dropped his mask, held up the bag and shook it; the rustle of candy wrappers was loud. "I'll be eating candy 'til Christmas!"

"Oh… good," she said unenthusiastically and straightened in her chair to get back to dealing with the business at hand. "Don't forget to check everything before you eat it," she called out absently, mind already focusing on the bills and checkbook in front of her. Was it her imagination or was the stack of bills actually higher this month? She shook her head; it was time to bite the bullet and dig in. She reached for the first unopened bill, slit the envelope, and pulled out the contents.

Suddenly: "Be right back! I forgot something!" And with that, he was gone, out the door before she could ask what he'd forgotten, or where he was going.

"Boys," she murmured, and glanced at the clock — not quite 7:00 yet, even though it was already dark. Still early enough. She turned her attention back to the bill, wrote down the balance and minimum payment, slipped it back into the envelope and set it aside. There was time to do this to a dozen or so bills before the front door slammed again. "Where were you?" she called, before he could even announce his return.

"I forgot Mrs. Bailey's," he explained, walking toward the kitchen. His footsteps were soft, cushioned by the soles of his costume.

"Mrs. Bailey?"

"The church lady." He was in the doorway to the kitchen, now, with a small, clear plastic bag. In it, a round loaf of bread about the size of two hands side by side was still warm enough to cause condensation on the inside of the bag. "You know, she makes the communion bread, and the kids get whatever's left over in Sunday school."

"Right — Mrs. Bailey."

"If she knows you, you get bread for a treat — and I almost forgot!" He peeled apart the seal at the top of the bag, reached in, and pulled the bread out. The scent of fresh-baked bread filled the kitchen almost immediately. It was a magical smell — at once it reminded her of church and communion — but also of home, and childhood, and her mother's fresh bread.

She took a deep breath, held the memories close, and then exhaled reluctantly. "I understand why you wanted to go back out."

"Who wouldn't? This is the best stuff in the world." He tore off a piece, offered it to his mother. "Want some?" She hesitated but a moment, then took it and bit off a smaller piece, let it sit on her tongue for a bit before she finally chewed slowly, letting the taste roll over her as the bread almost melted in her mouth. When that sensation started to fade, she took another bite, let it flow through her senses — smell, taste, texture…

If she could have heard it, it would have sounded like a choir of angels.

Her son took his own piece and then set the loaf aside. "You know," he said, "Halloween is my favorite holiday, and I really like trick-or-treating — but all of *that* stuff —" he tilted his head back toward the living room, where the sack of candy sat on the floor, "— I can't live on that. Sure, it tastes good when you first eat it, and it's sweet and all, but it doesn't fill you up, and after a while it just doesn't taste good."

He tore off another piece of bread, ate it slowly, speaking around it. "But this stuff, I could live on. I know we get the same bread at church every month, and it's the same bread she hands out for Halloween — but every time I eat it, it's like there's a different combination of flavors and how it feels. Sometimes it's crustier, sometimes it's saltier, or sweeter — but it's still the same. Do you know what I mean?"

"I think so," his mother said. "No matter how often you eat it, it's a little like the first time — but still familiar."

"Right. And it's *always* good." He offered another piece to her. "I know candy is good, but it's not good for me, and it's not real food. But this will always fill me up."

His mother took the piece and nodded. "That it will," she agreed. Then, gently, "Now why don't you get out of that costume? Your father will be home soon, and then we'll have dinner."

He smiled. "I may not be hungry by then."

After he left — with the bread — she sighed once more and turned back to the bills and budget... but suddenly it didn't seem quite as important. With the taste and smell of bread still lingering, and a warm fullness in her belly, it was hard to worry. Yes, the worries of life would be back soon enough.

But then there was always the bread...

About the Authors

David O. Bales was a Presbyterian (USA) pastor for 33 years, and is a graduate of the University of Portland (where he was editor of the yearbook) and San Francisco Theological Seminary. In addition to his ministry, he also has taught college: World Religions, Ethics, Biblical Hebrew and Biblical Greek (recently at College of Idaho). He has been a freelance researcher, writer, and editor for Stephen Ministries. His sermons and articles have appeared in *Interpretation*, *Pulpit Digest*, *Preaching*, *Lectionary Homiletics*, *Emphasis*, and *Preaching the Great Texts*. He wrote a year-long online column: "In The Original: Insights from Greek and Hebrew for the Lectionary Passages." His books include: *Gospel Subplots: Story Sermons of God's Grace*; *Toward Easter and Beyond*; *Scenes of Glory: Subplots of God's Long Story*; and *To the Cross and Beyond: Cycle A Sermons for Lent and Easter*, all available at CSS Publishing Company.

Scott Dalgarno is pastor of Wasatch Presbyterian Church in Salt Lake City, Utah. Born in California, he has previously served four Presbyterian churches in Oregon. He is a graduate of Whitworth University, University of Oregon, and San Francisco Theological Seminary. A poet, his poems have appeared in *The Christian Century*, *America*, *The Antioch Review*, and *Yale Review*.

Sandra Herrmann is a retired pastor and popular teacher in the Wisconsin Conference of the United Methodist Church. She is a poet and the author of *Ambassadors of Hope* (CSS). She has been published in *alive now!*, a magazine of spirituality of the UMC, *Emphasis* magazine for pastors, and currently writes monthly for *StoryShare*. She is working on a book exploring the Christian iconography of the Harry Potter series.

Keith Hewitt is the author of two volumes of *NaTiVity Dramas: Nontraditional Christmas Plays for All Ages* (CSS). He is a local pastor, co-youth leader, an occasional speaker at Christmas events, and former Sunday school teacher at Wilmot United Methodist Church in Wilmot, Wisconsin. He lives in southeastern Wisconsin with his wife, two children, and assorted dogs and cats.

Craig Kelly received his B.A. from the University of Saskatchewan in 2002. He and his wife, Beth, are actively involved in their church, working both in their church's children's ministry as well as working with low-income youth in their neighborhood. Craig enjoys reading, music, hiking, biking, and indulging in old sci-fi movies.

C. David McKirachan is pastor of the Presbyterian Church at Shrewsbury in central New Jersey. He also teaches at Monmouth University. McKirachan is the author of *I Happened Upon a Miracle* and *A Year of Wonder* (Westminster John Knox).

Rick McCracken-Bennett is an Episcopal priest, storyteller, writer, musician, and church planter. He is a member of the Storytellers of Central Ohio and the National Storytelling Network. His doctoral dissertation concerned the use of story to guide congregations into the future that God intends for them. He is the rector of All Saints Episcopal Church in New Albany, Ohio, where a sermon wouldn't be a sermon without a good story.

Stan Purdum, a United Methodist minister, is a freelance writer and editor. His books include *He Walked in Galilee*, about the ministry of Jesus (Abingdon Press, 2005) and *New Mercies I See*, short stories about God's grace (CSS Publishing Company, Inc., 2003), as well as four books about bicycling. He has been published in religious and secular journals, has authored numerous sermons for lectionary volumes and preaching journals, and writes adult Sunday school curriculum. Stan and his wife, Jeanine, live in North Canton, Ohio. They have three grown children.

Frank Ramirez has served as a pastor for nearly 30 years in Church of the Brethren congregations in Los Angeles, California; Elkhart, Indiana; and Everett, Pennsylvania. A graduate of LaVerne College and Bethany Theological Seminary, Ramirez is the author of numerous books, articles, and short stories. His CSS titles include *Partners in Healing*, *He Took a Towel*, *The Bee Attitudes*, and three volumes of *Lectionary Worship Aids*.

Argile Smith is Vice President for Advancement at William Carey University in Hattiesburg, Mississippi. He previously served at New Orleans Baptist Theological Seminary (NOBTS) as a preaching professor, chairman of the Division of Pastoral Ministries, and director of the communications center. While at NOTBS, Smith regularly hosted the Gateway to Truth program on the FamilyNet television network. He has also been the pastor of several congregations in Louisiana and Mississippi. Smith's articles have been widely published in church periodicals, and he is the author or editor of four books.

Peter Andrew Smith is an ordained minister in the United Church of Canada, currently serving St. James United Church in Antigonish, Nova Scotia. He is the author of *All Things Are Ready* (CSS), a book of lectionary-based communion prayers. He is also the author of a number of stories and articles, which can be found listed at www.peterandrewsmith.com.

The Rt. Rev. John S. Smylie, Bishop of Wyoming, previously served as the rector of St. Mark's Episcopal Church in Casper, Wyoming, and as the dean of the Cathedral of St. John the Evangelist in Spokane, Washington. He is a published author and storyteller as well as a singer-songwriter. Smylie recently completed *Grace for Today*, a collection of 25 stories that explores how grace, loss, and restoration are part of the same fabric.

John Sumwalt is the pastor of Our Lord's United Methodist Church in New Berlin, Wisconsin, and a noted storyteller. He is the author of nine books, including the acclaimed *Vision Stories* series and *How to Preach the Miracles: Why People Don't Believe Them and What You Can Do About It*. John and his wife Jo Perry-Sumwalt served for three years as the co-editors of *StoryShare*. A graduate of the University of Wisconsin-Madison and the University of Dubuque Theological Seminary (UDTS), Sumwalt received the Herbert Manning Jr. award for parish ministry from UDTS in 1997.

Larry Winebrenner graduated from Garrett Biblical Institute (now Garrett Evangelical Theological Seminary) over fifty years ago. He has been published in such varied publications as *The Christian Advocate*, *Games* magazine, and *Numismatic News*. He has been a contributor to *StoryShare* for a number of years. Larry served churches in Georgia, the Florida Keys, Indiana, and Wisconsin before returning to Miami, Florida, to teach at Miami-Dade College. He was an essential part of seeing the institution grow from a few classes held in a converted chicken coop to becoming the largest college in the United States of America. He now holds the title of Professor Emeritus from that institution.

If You Like This Book...

Please go to **www.csspub.com** or 800-241-4056 to order any of the below titles.

Some titles Stan Purdum has written and contributed to for CSS Publishing.

New Mercies I See
978-0-7880-1958-6 — printed book $12.95, e-book $9.95

Sermons on the First Readings, Series II, Cycle A
978-0-7880-2451-1 — printed book $37.95, e-book $29.95

Hear My Voice
978-0-7880-2400-9 — printed book $29.95, e-book $19.95

Leading to Easter: Sermon and Worship Resource
978-0-7880-1931-9 — printed book 11.95, e-book $8.95

Worship Resources for Special Sundays
978-0-7880-1974-6 — printed book $12.95, e-book $9.95

Christmas Treasures
978-0-7880-1976-0 — printed book $25.95, e-book $19.95

For other resources authored or contributed to by Stan Purdum, please visit www.csspub.com and type "Purdum" in the Search box option on the left hand side of the page.

Sandra Herrmann
Ambassadors of Hope
Second Reading Sermons for Lent and Easter, Cycle A
978-0-7880-0478-0 — printed book $9.95, e-book $7.95

John Smylie contributed to
Sermons on the Gospel Readings, Series III, Cycle B
"We Wish to See Jesus" for Lent/Easter
978-0-7880-2544-0 — printed book $37.95, e-book $29.95

Rick McCracken-Bennett contributed to
Sermons on the Gospel Readings, Series III, Cycle C
"Where Would You Go to Meet Jesus?"
middle third Pentecost
978-0-7880-2621-8 printed book $37.95, e-book $29.95

Peter Andrew Smith
All Things Are Ready
978-0-7880-2487-0 printed book $11.95, e-book $8.95

Keith Hewitt
NaTiVity Dramas
978-0-7880-2483-2 — printed book $12.95, e-book $9.95
NaTiVity Dramas the Second Season
978-0-7880-2641-6 — printed book $14.95, e-book $9.95
NaTiVity Dramas: The Third Season (978-0-7880-2695-9) will be released September 2012.

David O. Bales wrote
Scenes of Glory
978-0-7880-2554-9 — printed book $22.95, e-book $9.95

Sermons on the Second Readings, Series II, Cycle A
"Toward Easter and Beyond" for Lent/Easter
978-0-7880-2452-8 — printed book $37.95, e-book $29.95

For other resources authored or contributed to by David Bales, please visit www.csspub.com and type "Bales" in the Search box option on the left hand side of the page.

Some books John Sumwalt has written and/or edited for CSS Publishing.

How to Preach the Miracles, Cycle A
978-0-7880-2457-3 — printed book $19.95, e-book $9.95

Life Stories: Study in Christian Decision Making
978-0-7880-0330-1 — printed book $11.95, e-book $8.95

For other resources authored or edited by John Sumwalt, please visit www.csspub.com and type "Sumwalt" in the Search box option on the left hand side of the page.

Frank Ramirez has written and contributed to many different books for CSS Publishing.

Come All Ye Faithful
978-0-7880-2485-6 — printed book $8.95, e-book $6.95

Lectionary Worship Aids, Series VII, Cycle C
978-0-7880-2404-7 — printed book $24.95, e-book $19.95

Gabriel's Horn
978-0-7880-2385-9 — printed book $7.95, e-book $5.95

The Christmas Star
978-0-7880-1915-9 — printed book $9.95, e-book $7.95

For other resources authored or contributed to by Frank Ramirez, please visit www.csspub.com and type "Ramirez" in the Search box option on the left hand side of the page.

Argile Smith
Walking With God
Proper 23 Through Thanksgiving, First Readings, Cycle A
978-0-7880-2630-0 — printed book $12.95, e-book $9.95

Prices are subject to change without notice.

www.ingramcontent.com/pod-product-compliance
Ingram Content Group UK Ltd.
Pitfield, Milton Keynes, MK11 3LW, UK
UKHW021302180426
11947UKWH00015B/974